OPEN ROADS

About the Author

Photo by Costa Hadjilambrinos

Diane Thiel is the author of four books of poetry and prose: *Echolocations* (2000), which received the Nicholas Roerich Poetry Prize from Story Line Press; *Writing Your Rhythm: Using Nature, Culture, Form and Myth* (2001); *The White Horse: A Colombian Journey* (2004); and *Resistance Fantasies* (2004). Her work appears in numerous publications, including *Poetry, The Hudson Review,* and *Best American Poetry 1999,* and is reprinted in more than twenty major anthologies from Addison Wesley Longman, Bedford, HarperCollins, Beacon, Henry Holt, and McGraw Hill, including *Twentieth-Century American Poetry.* Her work has received numerous awards, including the Robert Frost Award and the Robinson Jeffers Award. Thiel received her BA and MFA from Brown University and has traveled and lived in various countries in Europe and South America. She has been a professor of creative writing for over ten years. Thiel was a Fulbright Scholar for 2001–2002 in Odessa, on the Black Sea, and is on the creative writing faculty at the University of New Mexico.

OPEN ROADS

Exercises
in Writing Poetry

Diane Thiel
University of New Mexico

PEARSON

Longman

New York San Francisco Boston
London Toronto Sydney Tokyo Singapore Madrid
Mexico City Munich Paris Cape Town Hong Kong Montreal

Managing Editor: Erika Berg
Development Manager: Janet Lanphier
Development Editor: Kristen Mellitt
Executive Marketing Manager: Ann Stypuloski
Production Manager: Eric Jorgensen
Project Coordination, Text Design, and Electronic Page Makeup: Electronic
    Publishing Systems Inc., NYC
Cover Designer/Manager: Wendy Ann Fredericks
Cover Art: Franz Marc, *Horse in a Landscape*, 1910. Oil painting on canvas,
    33 1/2 x 44 1/2. Museum Folkwang Essen.
Senior Manufacturing Buyer: Alfred C. Dorsey
Printer and Binder: RR Donnelley & Sons Company
Cover Printer: Coral Graphic Services, Inc.

For permission to use copyrighted material, grateful acknowledgment is made
to the copyright holders on pp. 227–229, which are hereby made part of this copyright page.

Library of Congress Cataloging-in-Publication Data

Thiel, Diane, [date]
Open roads : exercises in writing poetry / Diane Thiel.
    p. cm.
Includes bibliographical references and index.
ISBN 0-321-12760-9
1. English language—Rhetoric—Problems, exercises, etc. 2. Poetry—Author-
ship—Problems, exercises, etc. 3. Creative writing—Problems, exercises, etc.
4. Poetry—Collections. 5. College readers. I. Title.
PE1413.T448 2005
808.1—dc22
                                                                    2004018224

Visit us at http://www.ablongman.com.

ISBN 0-321-12760-9

2345678910—DOC—070605

For my mother
and the lineage of teachers
who inspired me to write

For writers who teach
For teachers who write

Contents

PART TWO
Exercises in Form
and Structure 87

PART THREE
A Collection of Readings   149

Preface to the Instructor

As teachers of poetry and creative writing, we face a unique challenge. The students in each of our courses have different talents and abilities. We must spark each student's creativity and help him or her develop the skills every competent writer must have. It is often said that creativity cannot be taught. It is my belief, however, that everyone possesses innate creativity, and it is our task, as teachers, to nourish it and give each student the means to express his or her ideas effectively. The teacher of the poetry workshop faces a set of specific challenges and needs a variety of tools in order to meet the needs of his or her students. Over many years of teaching and via discussions with a multitude of other teachers, I arrived at a list of tools most useful to a poetry writing classroom, tools featured in this book. The fundamental philosophy that this book embodies is that we learn by example and by practice. As writers, we are also readers, and we learn by emulating those poets who have most inspired us along the way. For this reason, the book includes an extensive selection of readings, and the exercises and discussions are designed to draw from and integrate with these readings.

Features of This Book

- Active lessons, with prompts to have the students writing something nearly every day.

- Exercises to address each element of poetry separately, while still building toward an understanding of all the elements that go into creating an effective poem.

- Clear, concise discussions of particular techniques of writing poetry, followed by practice of these individual techniques.

- Potent, vital examples in an extensive selection of readings that will serve as models to our students.

Open Roads: Exercises in Writing Poetry addresses the varied needs of the creative writing teacher. The purpose of this book is to make the process of writing poetry accessible and to help in the development of the necessary tools. The exercises identify and isolate the many elements of poetry, making them manageable. Thus broken down and explored one at a time, the elements of poetry become easier to handle. Some can be extraordinarily useful as steps on the way to longer pieces.

Though the exercises are designed to cover and respond to the fundamentals of poetry, they are also motivating and fun. Even as established writers, we set ourselves exercises. We study the techniques of other writers and often model a particular aspect of that writer's work (e.g., how the writer creates the rhythm in a free verse poem; how the perspective of a poem shifts at a particular moment).

Most of the selections in this book are from contemporary writers, although I do include a few classic pieces, often for the particular needs of an exercise, but also because it is important for students to get a sense of the lineage of writers. When Auden wrote his "Musée des Beaux Arts" in 1940, for example, he was "translating" a sixteenth-century Brueghel painting. Brueghel, in turn, referred quite precisely to the text of the ancient poet Ovid when he chose the figures for his painting. The readings represent writing in a number of different styles, from a number of different cultures and eras.

One important element that sets this book apart from other poetry writing textbooks is that the exercises throughout the book emphasize ways in which techniques that are primarily important to one genre can inform and enhance writing in other genres. When teaching poetry, I often take a passage of prose and examine the different "poetic" techniques that can be found there, such as parallel structures, metaphor, assonance, alliteration, or an underlying iambic or galloping anapestic rhythm. The techniques of writing dialogue, essential in fiction and drama, are also quite essential in narrative poetry. Emphasis on and examples of these types of connections appear throughout the book.

Organization: Ways to Use This Book

Part One of *Open Roads* will help students find their individual voices and begin addressing the elements of writing, such as voice, perspective, image, tension, and figurative language.

Part Two delves into specific concerns of form and structure, such as the nature of free verse, how to break a line, hearing the beat of a poem, and using rhyme.

Part Three is an anthology of poems that illustrates various points in the exercises, as well as a few poets' comments on the art. Suggestions for reading the pieces accompany many of the exercises in Parts One and Two. The readings also represent writing from a number of different cultures and eras.

You may choose to use the material in this book in the order of its appearance in the table of contents, but the exercises can also be used as the issues arise in workshop. For instance, as discussions arise regarding voice or perspective, you can turn to the exercises that address each particular concern and offer opportunities for practice. Often a work is suggested as a reading for a variety of different exercises. Revisiting the selections a number of times, to study different aspects of a writer's technique, will give students good examples for emulation and will get them in the habit of "reading as a writer."

Examples of Exercises

As a professor of poetry and creative writing for the last twelve years, and as an author of books of poetry and prose, I have developed hundreds of exercises that focus on particular elements of creative writing crucial for any poet's development. These include exercises addressing such concerns as establishing perspective, creating images and symbols, depicting culture and history, developing a narrative, and attending to form. I approach the essential tools of poetry in ways that make each point relevant to the student's own experiences.

The exercises include opportunities to address specific as well as more expansive elements of poetry. Some work well as fifteen-minute free-writing exercises, while others can be used as inspiration for an assignment at home.

The exercises will motivate students and give teachers brief daily lessons for discussion, as well as offer hands-on exercises to follow. Another emphasis of the book is the process of revision. The revision exercises give ideas and present ways to approach revision, and they include a set of questions that can be used in any workshop of student work.

As mentioned previously, most readings in this book are modern and contemporary, although a few classic readings are chosen particularly because they illustrate effectively certain elements of creative writing and because they give rise to interesting and playful exercises. For instance, the inclusion of Coleridge's "Kubla Kahn" leads to an exercise in which students write a collaborative completion of the poem. The dreamlike, organic nature of Coleridge's "unfinished fragment" allows for a fun exercise in catching the rhythm of a piece, as well as accessing first thoughts. (For instance, Coleridge's fragment ends in "For he on honeydew hath fed / and drunk the milk of paradise." Students might follow with a line such as "And then he ate a cantaloupe.")

This book addresses, in creative new ways, aspects of writing that some instructors have found most difficult to teach—poetic meter for instance. For example, one exercise asks students to emulate an eight-line passage from Shakespeare's *Macbeth*. We study the way the iambic meter of the play shifts to trochaic meter for the casting of the witches' spell and the effect this shift creates. Students then emulate the meter and write spells in trochaic meter, using the witches' spell as a template. This type of exercise (useful in helping the student grasp the concept) is then followed by freer exercises in the particular technique. The book also includes exercises that bring other arts such as music or painting into the conversation in order to better understand the written piece or exercise, while simultaneously emphasizing the connections between different genres, different media, and different eras.

Included in the pages that follow are exercises I have found to be useful in the classroom as well as to my own creative development. As you travel through this book, either in the order of the table of contents or by moving around as the need in workshop arises, I hope you will be inspired to create additional exercises of your own and to find sources of inspiration for your own writing.

Acknowledgments

I would like to thank my thousands of students and many colleagues over the years, as well as the creative writing instructors who reviewed the manuscript in progress: Jennifer Atkinson, George Mason University; Thomas Fox Averill, Washburn University of Topeka; Philip Heldrich, Emporia State University; John S. Nelson, Dakota State University; Joy Passanante, University of Idaho; D. K. Peterson, North Dakota State University; Sheryl St. Germaine, Iowa State University; Keith Taylor, University of Michigan; and Eric Torgerson, Central Michigan University. I am grateful to Joe Terry, Erika Berg, Kristen Mellitt, and Dana Gioia for their assistance at various stages in the process. Thanks to my mother (an inspiring teacher for forty-five years) and all the members of my family. As always, many thanks to my husband, Costa, for his extraordinary assistance at every stage of the writing of this book.

DIANE THIEL

Introduction

If you have opened this book even in curiosity, you have at least wondered about becoming a writer. The idea of writing to be read may be exciting, scary, or both. These feelings are natural, especially if you have not had much experience with it. Whether you have had much practice with writing or little, you should know that you are already a writer. You are an observer of life and a story-teller, even if you don't immediately think of yourself that way. When something exciting happens in your life, what is one of your first impulses? To tell someone else. This is true for every one of us. We tell stories all our lives and use them daily for entertainment, to give advice, to make community.

As an observer and a story-teller, you are always looking and listening, consciously or unconsciously, for points of inspiration, and this attention becomes heightened when you start putting your ideas down on the page. It is usually this step, beginning to put your ideas on paper, that seems the most difficult to take. Beginning the process of writing, however, is easier than you may think. The first step is to keep a journal, and, as the first exercise in this book shows, writing in your journal is really no more difficult than observing or imagining a few things that may later become points of departure for a piece.

Although being a writer is as natural as being able to talk, to run, or to throw, being an *effective* writer is no different from being an effective singer or athlete. You must sharpen and improve your natural abilities and reflexes. There is no better way to do this as a writer than by reading widely and trying out the techniques of writers you admire. T. S. Eliot once commented (though he may have stolen it from Ezra Pound), "Good poets borrow. Great poets steal." The real art is in finding the way to emulate something so as to make it your own.

The poetic tradition stretches back to ancient times, and it can be inspiring to recognize ourselves as an extension of that rich and diverse lineage. This book will point out many roads you can take as a writer. It is an exciting process to see your writing as an extension of that ancient path, with an open road and a unique landscape of possibilities unfolding before you.

When we write poetry, we tap into a wellspring that is the source of all the arts and that reflects the breadth of our human experience. In this book, we will explore different sources of inspiration, such as music, myth, history, and art, in the making of a poem. If we look back in history to the early roots of writing, we can recognize the deep connections between

1

our more recent divisions, such as poetry, drama, story, history, and song. They all stem from the same source and once co-existed in our ancient texts.

You will find in this book a collection of exercises that address the elements of writing essential to poetry. The exercises set simple tasks, the objectives of which are to help you practice your technique. They provide simultaneous inspiration and a delving into particular concerns of poetry.

This book also suggests ways in which techniques that are primarily important to poetry can inform and enhance your writing in other forms. For instance, your fiction can be enhanced by the attention to language and rhythm that poetry provides. If you look closely at a passage of good prose, you can notice the different poetic techniques the author has used, such as parallel structures, metaphor, alliteration, or even an underlying iambic or other notable rhythm (all elements discussed in these pages). The techniques of writing dialogue, essential in fiction, are also quite essential in narrative poetry.

You will also discover important connections between all the creative arts that can help you more clearly understand the elements of creative writing. Hemingway commented that he learned about writing through his love of certain composers and their music and learned "as much from painters about how to write as from writers." Discussion of these types of connections is an important element of this book.

Whether you are a beginning or more experienced writer, it is important to begin each piece by breaking it down into a number of small explorations. This process of breaking down, or, alternatively, of beginning with small pieces that you may later synthesize into a larger one, is useful because it makes the task of writing easier to manage and helps you learn by isolating each element of your piece. As you focus your attention on each element, you are better able to determine how you can improve it. One of the greatest questions you will face as a writer is how you are going to *render*, cast or shape, your piece. The idea that sparks a work is important, of course, but, as Robert Frost writes, "how you say a thing" is what ultimately matters in writing.

Often a terrific idea can feel too huge to handle. Many extraordinary ideas remain, unfortunately, at the idea stage. The exercises in this book will help you break down the elements of poetry into small ventures that will teach you about the art. All works, no matter how large, are composed in such pieces: a scene, an extended metaphor, a line. As the poet and novelist Kate Braverman says, "All good writing is built one good line at a time.... One word, one stone at a time." You always need to address each small component, however expansive the work might become.

The adage about activism applies in writing as well: "Think globally. Act locally." While it is always necessary that you maintain a global vision of the scope and purpose of your piece, this vision can be realized most effectively by paying close local attention to and carefully crafting each word, line, and element of the piece.

All writers learn by reading and by setting themselves exercises. This process of sharpening your tools and honing your techniques is necessary in the same way that ongoing training is necessary for an athlete, a musician, a visual artist. I encourage you to return to the exercises and the readings at different stages and to read widely beyond the sample of works included in the book. In fact, what you can learn from the exercises and readings grows and changes as your technique develops.

The art of poetry, of course, as any art, is more than just exercise. The poet Rainer Maria Rilke, in his "Letter to a Young Poet," refers to the true source of the art when he says, "I know of no other advice than this: Go within and scale the depths." Although there are no formulas that will assure you will write a great poem, there are techniques you can develop and practice which will help you truly "scale the depths."

PART ONE

Exercises
for Developing Craft
and Technique

1
Beginning:
Points of Inspiration

Keeping a Journal

Keeping a journal is an indispensable part of being a writer. In a sense, your memory is your journal. The point of both is to record things such as events, thoughts, sensations, and dreams. But as we all know, memory constantly discards details, and that is why it is good practice to keep a written journal. It may even be a good idea to keep more than one. Thoreau, for instance, kept different volumes for his scientific observations and his ideas for literary pieces, but he noted that it became increasingly difficult for him to keep things separate.

Though our technology has developed a multitude of machines to help us write, from recorders to computers to voice recognition systems, there is still no better way for you to begin than writing by hand. You can and should, of course, type things later, as you begin to revise, but it is important that you get started with your pen on paper. The immediate and direct physicality of forming words on the page cannot be substituted because it offers the closest connection between the writing process and its raw material, the word.

The shape and size of your journal are also important. It has to be small enough to carry in your purse or backpack, yet large enough to write in comfortably and fluidly. You should be able to carry it with you conveniently everywhere you go. You might consider your journal as your enhanced memory and write in it everything that can conceivably be of use to you later. And considering that you never know ahead of time what will be useful, the category of things you write in your journal could be very broad: dreams, quotations, overheard bits of dialogue.

Be prepared to "throw away" ninety-five percent of your writing—or rather, let it go no further than your journal. You will often write ten lines to get a single good one. Think of the journal as a no-pressure situation. There is never a blank page to face, because your hand keeps moving.

Of course, journal entries are far from final pieces. Writers often walk around with an idea for many years—a great idea that hasn't quite found its form, or its connecting force. "Free-writing" (keeping the hand moving, without censoring or revising for the moment) in a journal can help you find these connections, as you record the ebb and flow of your thoughts. Practically speaking, the journal is a convenient way of keeping thoughts and ideas organized and safe from being lost.

When you are feeling somewhat uninspired, you can turn to the pages in your journal for instantaneous sparks of creativity. You will hardly remember writing some of the things that made it into the pages.

Suggestions for Writing

1. If you don't already have a journal, begin one and record in it such things as:

   Your dream last night

   Quotations from things you are reading

   Overheard snippets of conversation

   Intriguing scientific facts

   An interesting name for a character

   Something unusual you saw on the way home

2. If you have been keeping a journal for a while, revisit some old entries. Open your journal at a random place and read a few pages. Pick a thought, an idea, an image, and explore it from your current perspective. Write a new entry that revisits an old theme.

Personal Stories:
History as Heartbeat

Researching history can be a way to access the past and connect it to the present and the future. But the research has to mean something. It has to become personal. "History is your own heartbeat," as the poet Michael S. Harper says. History, especially your personal history, is a fundamental source and shaper of your ideas. So go ahead and mine it.

Read/Revisit

Miller Williams, "The Curator" (see page 219)

Suggestions for Writing

1. Choose an ancestor who has always interested you, and do some research on historical events that took place during his or her life. Do some personal research. Interview your family members about family history. Record what you hear in your journal. You may find that the story you are seeking has always been at your fingertips.

2. Start by writing about a single incident in your ancestor's life. It might be hard to get started if you think you have to tell a whole life story. So just start with one story: a story the family still tells, one that survived via the oral tradition. This might be a defining moment in the ancestor's life, or a story he or she might tell (or has told) you.

3. Write a three to five page biography of your ancestor. Focus on specific details.

Memory and Imagination

Memory is the source of imagination. What we think of, regardless of how imaginative or whimsical, is in one way or another based on what we know. The inventive use of memory is an integral aspect of the creative process. We all remember things differently, so the very act of reconstructing the past is always a creative one. The details we include and the details we exlude help to form our own personal version of events.

Read/Revisit

> Theodore Roethke, "My Papa's Waltz" (see page 206)
> Judith Ortiz Cofer, "Quinceañera" (see page 166)

Suggestions for Writing

1. Think of your earliest memory. As you write about it, try to inhabit the voice of the child. You might incorporate nonsense words to enhance the effect of the particular age. Note how Roethke's poem "My Papa's Waltz" presents the speaker's memory of his father. What details help capture the child's perspective? Try to recreate similar details.

2. Write a memory of something you couldn't possibly remember: your grandparents' wedding, your birth, the creation of the earth.

3. Write about a memory of a significant life event or rite of passage, as Judith Ortiz Cofer does in "Quinceañera" (the celebration when girls in her culture turn fifteen).

Telling Lies to Tell the Truth

As children, we are all told not to lie, yet, much of our lives, we end up telling lies: tiny, harmless, "white" lies, perhaps, but lies nonetheless. In telling "white" lies, though, we often deny our true selves. Creative writing, on the other hand, is often all about making up stories. It gives us license to tell huge lies. We can invent personas, embody our dreams, tell the tallest of tales. In fact, the taller they are, sometimes the more true they become on the page. We can reveal much of our true selves when we invent personas through which to speak, or create metaphor. It could be said that all figurative language is, in a sense, a lie, because it presents one thing as something else. Yet it so often has the effect of getting closer to the truth. (See the "Figurative Language" chapter for more specifics.)

Suggestions for Writing

1. This exercise is a good one to access the true events of your life that are strange enough to sound like lies. Write three short statements or anecdotes about yourself: two lies and one truth, with the same level of believability. In a workshop, it can be fun to read your responses aloud and let others guess which is the truth.

2. Write about fifty words telling an absolute lie that somehow is true to the way you feel.

   For instance, one student wrote about her Spanish teacher vanishing into thin air. Perhaps the student was wishing her away, or perhaps she was turning to magic realism (where reality suddenly becomes fantastic).

Random Connections

Read/Revisit

> Lawrence Ferlinghetti, "Don't Let That Horse Eat That Violin" (see page 174)

Elizabeth Bishop got her inspiration for the poem "The Man-Moth" from a misprint for "mammoth" in a newspaper. Typographical, grammatical, or foreign-language translation errors can be a great source of inspiration. I have saved them for years, from various sources:

- A sign in a Paris hotel elevator: *Please leave your values at the front desk.*

- A wrong answer on a high school science test: H_2O *is hot water.* CO_2 *is cold water.*

A student in one of my classes repeated the phrase "as I lied in bed last night" several times in a writing assignment. I couldn't resist asking her in the margin whom she was lying to.

Use these mishaps as leaping off points. In *Leaping Poetry*, Robert Bly refers to the "long floating leap . . . from the conscious to the unconscious." Writing is very much about the accidental connection, and about allowing these connections to occur. I am reminded of Lawrence Ferlinghetti's poem about Chagall:

> Don't let that horse
> eat that violin
> cried Chagall's mother
> But he
> kept right on
> painting

An important element in all good writing is fresh, innovative *diction* (word choice) and *syntax* (arrangement of words). The source of the right word is sometimes one of those mysterious, elusive elements of writing. Sometimes the right word arrives as a gift. Found poems and other serendipitous exercises help charge the imagination with new combinations.

Suggestions for Writing

1. "Found poems" are poems that are literally found (whole or almost in their entirety) in unexpected places. Try finding a poem in your belongings: the ingredients on a candy bar, the fine print on an I.D., a page of your chemistry book, a funny or disturbing memo you received at work, an overheard conversation. First, stick

as close to the original as you can. You might find that you have an entire poem, or it might become the kernel of something more elaborate, perhaps an element of a story.

2. "Random connections" is a fun exercise and a good game. Participants should break into sets of two. Without consulting each other, one person should come up with a "Why?" The other should come up with a "Because." Some of the links work beautifully. Others are bizarre, but they might work even more beautifully. You could try this exercise with other links: if, then; I used to, but now. The following are several examples from students:

Why do I see the things I see in your eyes?
Because the T.V. is on.

Why do we wear clothes?
Because we feel like dancing.

Why do I have to grow up?
Because you broke it.

If frogs ruled the world,
then birds would swim.

I used to be afraid of the dark,
But now I can't see a thing.

I used to fall in love at the drop of a pin,
But now I sleep with my eyes open.

I used to think my teachers weren't human,
But now I can drive.

3. Refrigerator magnet words can be useful for sparking ideas (and you can use them while making dinner). Even self-proclaimed nonwriters have found them inspiring. In a workshop, you could also use word lists or cards. Make lists or piles of nouns, verbs, adjectives, etc., and then pick from the piles to see what constructions result. You could select consciously, or you might close your eyes and pick randomly. It is rare, of course, that a whole poem or story will emerge from such serendipitous exercises, but perhaps a new image or idea will appear. I confess that occasionally a line from my refrigerator finds its way into a piece of writing.

2
Voice and Tone

Finding Your True Subjects

Read/Revisit

Elizabeth Bishop, "One Art" (see page 161)

Your choice (or discovery) of subjects is one factor that will begin to define your voice. Often, our true subjects may very well be the wounds or difficulties we have undergone. In a way, your subject chooses you. You may not want a certain subject matter, but it is yours anyway, because it is something you may need to work through for a period of time, or even for the rest of your life.

Elizabeth Bishop, for instance, began dealing with the subject of lost things early in her life. The use of the villanelle form for "One Art" is particularly intriguing, because the form of repetition lends itself well to subject matters that are, in a way, one's obsessions.

Suggestions for Writing

1. Look through your journals. Do any subjects appear again and again? Has someone ever pointed out to you that you talk about the same thing? Often, the word *obsession* has negative connotations, but for writers, obsessions can be the mark of having found a true subject.

2. Keep a dream journal. A true subject might be revealed by the frequency with which you dream about it. Record your dreams for a few weeks. Write down what you remember immediately on waking.

3. Experiment with refrains. See if one of your subject matters would benefit from one of the forms of repetition in poetry. (See Part Two for more specifics.)

Embodying a Voice

Read/Revisit

Miller Williams, "The Curator" (see page 219)

Miller Williams has commented that he wrote "The Curator" after overhearing a Hermitage employee tell the story of what happened at the museum during the siege of Leningrad (now St. Petersburg) in World War II. In the poem, Williams assumes the voice of the curator and tells the story in the first person. In this way, he can relate the experiences, thoughts, and feelings of the curator in an immediate and direct way, giving the story a vibrancy it might not otherwise have.

Suggestions for Writing

1. Think of a story you have overheard someone tell. Or make it a deliberate exercise to listen for pieces of conversation. Record what you overhear someone say.

   Write through that person's perspective. Try to capture the tone and style of the speaker's voice. In "The Curator," for instance, note how the speaker keeps moving deeper and deeper into the point of the story, by such breaks in the text that suggest "here, here is the story I want to tell."

2. Narrate a story in which the true identity of the narrator is concealed until close to the end of the piece. For instance, you might write a piece in which the narrator appears to be a jealous girlfriend, bothered by a female visitor, but in the end, it becomes clear that the speaker is actually the cat.

Shifting Tone

Read/Revisit

> Theodore Roethke, "My Papa's Waltz" (see page 206)
> Wendy Cope, "Lonely Hearts" (see page 167)
> Diane Thiel, *"Memento Mori* in Middle School" (see page 213)

Theodore Roethke's poem has, in some ways, an elusive tone. It might be read with an introspective, light tone, a memory of one's father. However, a number of readers find the poem rather dark, and find that the choice of words and details such as the belt scraping the child's ear give the poem a somewhat ominous tone.

In "Lonely Hearts," Wendy Cope uses romance ads as a basis for her form of repetition, the villanelle. Is the tone playful? Do you also feel some degree of longing, or loneliness? Note how a piece might convey two rather different tones at once.

The poem *"Memento Mori* in Middle School" seems to have a playful tongue-in-cheek tone (with the child's interpretation of Dante's *Inferno*) but details are introduced later in the poem, in the "wood of suicides" for instance, that convey a much heavier tone.

Suggestions for Writing

Choose a subject, like Roethke's memory of his father, for which you could create two different tones. What would the two tones be? What details might you include to establish each particular tone? Write a short freewrite using one of the tones. Then try the other.

3
Perspective, Point of View, and Distance

Choosing Points of View

Some years back, I had the opportunity to take a canoe trip through one of South Florida's cypress forests with some friends, among them a botanist and an ornithologist. To the botanist, the trip was an exciting exploration of the overabundant plant life of the area. Her eye sought the epiphytes growing on the limbs of the tall trees, the vines fighting their way over almost every stump, and the flowers proclaiming the presence of both rare and common species. Not only was she able to identify each plant, but her training allowed her to use clues such as their relative abundance and position to see the state of the ecosystem as we passed through it. To the ornithologist, on the other hand, the forest we were passing through consisted primarily of sounds. Although the birds were mostly hidden in the branches, he was able to identify them through their calls. He could even interpret the calls: mating song, cry of alarm, and so on. Were both to be asked to describe the trip, each would come up with a very different account—each description shaped by the education, experience, and interests of the narrator. The differences in their *perspectives* would give rise to two very different versions.

The perspective from which you choose to tell a story is an essential element of the narrative because it determines what you can reveal about the situation, the characters, and the action, what position you take regarding these things, which details you will focus on and which you will omit, and so on. Perspective is such an integral part of a story that very often it is absolutely clear whose story this is, so there really is no choice to be made about it. Nevertheless, it is always useful to maintain a critical attitude, or distance, about all elements of the narrative. By challenging even as fundamental an aspect as perspective, by trying out different alternatives, you can be sure that you do not miss an opportunity to strengthen your piece by, for example, choosing a perspective that could offer an unexpected insight.

Suggestions for Writing

1. In an earlier exercise, you wrote about your earliest memory. Now take that memory and tell the same story from a variety of different perspectives (e.g., your own, your mother's, your grandfather's). Continue to use first person.

2. You wrote the earliest memory using first-person point of view. Now write the same memory using third person (refer to yourself as "he" or "she").

3. Imagine a dramatic setting for your character (a battlefield, a courtroom, a family dinner), and write a brief speech for the character in which he or she is trying to convince his or her audience to take some action. Write in first-person plural (using "we").

4. Now try the less common second-person point of view (using "you" or the implied "you"). Think of a point in your life when you had to obey someone or follow that person's instructions and advice for much of your day (as you would in the army, your childhood home, a classroom, a sports team). Describe an incident or a day using only a list of instructions, orders, or admonitions.

5. In his poem, "The Whipping," Robert Hayden shifts from third person ("his") to first person ("my") in the middle of the poem. In the first half of the poem, Hayden, as an outside observer describes the scene of a boy being beaten by his mother. Then, Hayden shifts to the first person and identifies with the boy who is being punished.

   Try a piece that starts out using one point of view and then shifts to a different one for a particular effect.

Innocent Perspective

A newcomer in a society has a unique perspective because of an unfamiliarity with certain linguistic and social conventions. He or she has to deduce meaning from what is observable. There is much we can learn by looking at familiar things with a new perspective. This innocent view has the power to illuminate something obvious but hidden to most observers. Children, for instance, in their naiveté, are often the ones who reveal that the emperor has no clothes.

Writing from a perspective other than one's own can be mind-broadening. It is even more challenging to write about one's own culture through that other perspective. Our daily rituals, as common as they are to us, would seem bizarre to another culture, just as other cultures' rituals often strike us as strange. We have all opened *National Geographic* and been fascinated by the "necks wound round and round with wire," as Elizabeth Bishop says in her poem "In the Waiting Room." But how would our own daily rituals seem to an outsider: acts as common as shaving or applying make-up? What might other cultures think of plastic surgery? It is certainly no less bizarre as a cultural practice than the scarification rituals of certain African tribes, which shock us when we see them depicted in magazines or on television.

We have seen the use of an innocent perspective in mainstream media, in popular TV shows and movies like *Third Rock from the Sun* and *Look Who's Talking*. I have a favorite moment in the movie *Starman*, when the alien has observed and quickly assessed the rules of driving. He says, "I understand. Red means stop. Green means go. Yellow means go very very fast." He misunderstands the rules but reveals a truth we all recognize.

Read/Revisit

Craig Raine, "A Martian Sends a Postcard Home" (see page 202)

It can be liberating to write from the "limited perspective" of an alien. Craig Raine's "A Martian Sends a Postcard Home" is a good example in its depiction of such common items as a clock and a phone. Raine's poem takes on various aspects of contemporary daily life, but it just touches the surface of possibility.

Suggestions for Writing

1. Imitate Raine and explore various aspects of twenty-first-century America through the perspective of an alien. Try writing a poem like Raine's, or you might want to construct a narrative. Or you could write an analytical piece, a report on your findings. Writing from an alien perspective allows satire of many different aspects of human

society. You could focus on a bar, a nuclear waste disposal site, a landfill, a school, a jail, a factory, a stripclub, a battlefield. It is a useful way to shake up your own notions about the society in which you live, to look at it with new eyes, the eyes of an outsider who may misunderstand and, in doing so, reveal a deeper truth.

2. This exercise is a variation of the one above, as it brings up the assumptions archeologists make about past cultures. Imagine yourself arriving on a desolate, uninhabited Earth in some future year. Write through the perspective of an archeologist, digging up the objects of our everyday lives. Focus on the symbolic value of the objects you find. What do they suggest about the culture that lived here? What assumptions can you make about a society that leaves behind the golden arches of McDonald's and a landfill full of Styrofoam? What might a high-heeled shoe, make-up, and a bikini say about the society? Write an assessment of some aspect of twenty-first-century America based on the items that you find.

Using Biography

Read/Revisit

Hart Crane, "My Grandmother's Love Letters" (see page 168)
Sor Juana, "She Promises to Hold a Secret in Confidence" (see page 209)

Suggestions for Writing

1. In an earlier exercise, you wrote a biography of a family member or an ancestor. Now narrate a single incident through the voice of the person in the biography. Don't take on too much at once. Choose a dramatic moment of this person's life as a focal point of the narration.

   Sometimes writing with a different voice allows us to explore aspects about ourselves we might not otherwise reveal. And it can allow us to come closer to someone else's experience.

2. Narrate a historical event either from the perspective of a participant or an observer.

3. Write a letter from an ancestor's perspective. Or, if you have any actual old correspondence, use it as a source of inspiration, as in Hart Crane's "My Grandmother's Love Letters":

   > There is even room enough
   > For the letters of my mother's mother,
   > Elizabeth,
   > That have been pressed so long
   > Into a corner of the roof. . . .

   > And I ask myself:

   > "Are your fingers long enough to play
   > Old keys that are but echoes . . . ?"

4
Selecting Details

Detailing a Poem

As the saying goes, the devil is in the details, and it's true. Think of the world as made up of countless little pieces, the details our senses perceive. There are just too many to include when we describe something in writing. So when we write, we must choose which details are most crucial to the story we are trying to tell or the scene we are trying to depict. We must choose carefully and deliberately because the choice of what we include and what we omit establishes the mood, tone, and direction of our piece.

Suggestions for Writing

1. Describe a character by the things in that individual's purse, briefcase, desk, office. Let these details reveal something about the character.

2. Try selecting details that appeal to senses other than vision. What difference is created by the details of the scent of roses as opposed to a visual description of a rosebush? Describe, for instance, the kitchen of the home you grew up in via the smells you remember.

3. Establish a setting or character. List every detail you can come up with. Now try to select from the list. Which details might have symbolic value and function on more than one level (e.g., a heat wave, which might also imply passion or anger brimming beneath the surface)? Which details help reveal something about the character or setting without stating it directly (e.g., a fur coat and diamonds)?

Place with Personality

Read/Revisit

William Stafford, "Traveling through the Dark" (see page 210)

An important question for the writer to answer early on is "Where are we, and when?" Readers generally need the details of a concrete setting in order to "enter" a piece and imagine themselves in it. Sometimes the title helps to place the reader in space and time. Notice, in Stafford's poem, how we know where we are from the first lines.

Though in most creative writing the setting is concrete (i.e., represents a specific time and place), in some cases, especially in poetry, the setting might describe purely a state of mind—thoughts or emotions. Other times, the setting is a dream world, as in Coleridge's "Kubla Khan." In all these cases, however, the setting is both specific and an essential element.

Suggestions for Writing

1. Choose a limited setting and write about it. Try to select an area or a place that might have symbolic resonance on a number of levels (a church, your grandmother's attic, a cabin in the woods).

    In a workshop, you might also all come up with ideas for evocative settings and then decide on a single one. Each person should then write a few opening lines reflecting the same place. It would be interesting to read these aloud and hear how much they differ in tone, or perhaps don't, depending on the setting selected and the different contexts.

2. Write a poem that takes place in a dream, or an essay about a dream you hope could become real. Describe how the world would be if your dream were realized.

3. Create a scenario and describe the aspects of your setting in terms of a character. Try not to use a cliché like "the angry sea," although you may certainly describe the ways in which the sea is angry.

5
Image and Symbol

Turning Abstractions into Images

One old adage of writing bears repeating: "Show, don't just tell." A little "telling" (or expository discussion about the matter) is sometimes essential, but it shouldn't merely restate or replace the image, and it should be kept in balance with the "showing" (the vivid details). Specificity can actually have a far greater power of universality than vague abstractions. If you write, for instance, about one very specific loss and inhabit the experience with vivid, descriptive language, it will have more far-reaching effects than if you speak about loss in the abstract. Note Elizabeth Bishop's treatment of loss in "One Art."

Read/Revisit

Elizabeth Bishop, "One Art" (see page 161)
April Lindner, "Spice" (see page 195)

Suggestions for Writing

1. Use an earlier piece of class writing to find examples of abstractions that could be made concrete. Or write down several abstract words, such as several emotions (anger, happiness, etc.) or any words ending in *ism*. Then use an image or series of images to convey each abstraction. For example, for anger, one might depict a red face or a muscle in the temple twitching. If you are in a workshop, you could scramble and exchange your abstract words with other participants.

2. Note how Bishop depicts loss, ranging from lost door keys to lost continents to a lost love. The poem's list builds in intensity. Write down an abstract idea, such as "loss." Then make a list of specific details that might convey the abstract idea.

3. List a few abstract concepts (e.g., domesticity, longing, love). Now replace them with a common household object, as Lindner does in "Spice." Write a short piece with the common object as its focus. Don't state the abstract concept in your piece.

27

Using All of Your Senses

All good creative writing is based on sensory experience. We often think of images as being visual, but they can be auditory, tactile, olfactory, and gustatory as well. Good imagery reveals something with new eyes and ears and hands and turns it around for examination, as in these words from Mariane Moore's "Poetry":

> . . .The bat,
> holding on upside down or in quest of something to
> eat, elephants pushing, a wild horse taking a roll, a tireless wolf under
> a tree, the immovable critic twinkling his skin like a horse that
> feels a flea . . .

Consider Ezra Pound's poem "In a Station of the Metro":

> The apparition of these faces in the crowd;
> Petals on a wet, black bough.
>
> EZRA POUND (1885–1972)

Although every good writer uses imagery, the above poems are examples of "Imagist" poetry. The Imagists flourished particularly from 1908 to 1917 and included such poets as Wallace Stevens, William Carlos Williams, H. D. (Hilda Doolittle), Carl Sandburg, Ezra Pound, and Marianne Moore. Pound first wrote his famous two-line poem as a thirty-line piece, but he found that the "one-image" poem captured more than a page of words in this case—a single, almost cinematic image (slowed down by the "apparition") that would reverberate afterwards. He thought of the poem as "haiku-like."

Read/Revisit

William Butler Yeats, "The Lake Isle of Innisfree" (see page 225)
Marianne Moore, "Poetry" (see page 197)

Suggestions for Writing

1. Practice the "single image." Write a series of haiku-like poems. Now try incorporating the image in a short paragraph. How does it affect the paragraph to have begun with the heightened image?
2. Try creating imagery using senses other than vision. Let us hear the "lake water lapping" and the "bee-loud glade," as in Yeats's "Lake Isle of Innisfree." (see page 225)

Writing from Art

Read/Revisit

W. H. Auden, "Musée des Beaux Arts" (see page 160)
William Carlos Williams, "The Dance" (see page 222)

Note the way in which Auden's poem "Musée des Beaux Arts" is a translation of Brueghel's painting *The Fall of Icarus*. In the same manner, Brueghel used the text of the first-century Roman poet Ovid when he painted his *Icarus* in the 1500s. References to the ploughman, the fisher, and the shepherd appear in the ancient text. It is also interesting to note that the rhythms of Williams's "The Dance" mimic the rhythms of a dance. (The rhythm in this poem is discussed more extensively in the "Free Verse" and "Rhythm and Refrain" chapters in Part Two.)

All forms of art essentially do the same thing: they explore the nuances of the human experience. It is not surprising, then, that artists working in one form often draw inspiration from works of art in other forms. The connection between literature and painting is particularly strong, perhaps because of the vivid imagery both art forms employ.

Writing from art, known as *ekphrastic* writing, is a great way to hone your sense of the image.

The Fall of Icarus by Pieter Brueghel the Elder (1520?–1569)
Source: Scala/Art Resource, NY

Suggestions for Writing

1. Visit a museum or an art gallery. Or spend some time in a library or bookstore looking through some books with photographs of works of art. Write a response to a work of art that moves you because of its subject or imagery. When you travel and visit museums, carry your journal with you. Wandering through a gallery usually fills you with rich images and inspiration.

2. Give someone a voice: choose someone or something in a painting or sculpture. Write a short piece—a dialogue, an essay, a poem, or a story—from his, her, or its perspective.

3. Riff on a work of art. What does a particular painting make you think about? Where does it send you?

   Write a piece that focuses on a seemingly obscure detail in the piece of art—a cat on the windowsill in the background, for instance.

Making Metaphor

Read/Revisit

Richard Wilbur, "The Writer" (see page 218)
Wallace Stevens, "Disillusionment of Ten O'Clock" (see page 211)
John Ashbery, "Paradoxes and Oxymorons" (see page 159)
Robert Frost, "Poetic Metaphor" from "Education by Poetry" (see page 178)

The word *metaphor* comes from the Greek, meaning "to carry over." In Greece, I noticed that moving trucks bear the word *Metafores* on the side. The mind organizes material by trying to link something new to what it already knows. It wants to make metaphor. Essentially, when using metaphor, we speak about one thing in terms of something else. We use metaphor many times a day, without even realizing it.

Sometimes, as I begin to talk about the term in a class and ask the class to give me a metaphor, students sit searching their minds until someone finally comes up with a meager one. Yet they have all probably used several rich ones in their last conversation. Metaphor fills our language, from our daily accounts to our insults to our terms of endearment.

Robert Frost, in his essay "Education by Poetry," suggests that poetry plays an important role in the development of thinking. He discusses the importance of analogy in reasoning and emphasizes the practical nature of using metaphor, how we learn to link one thing to another. This kind of association challenges our minds and builds associative muscles. Aristotle (384–322 B.C.) believed that metaphor (the word is sometimes used to mean all figurative language) was the most important skill of an educated person. He wrote:

> By far the greatest thing is to be a master of metaphor. It is the one thing that cannot be learned from others. It is a sign of genius, for a good metaphor implies an intuitive perception of similarity among dissimilars.

Although Aristotle may have been right in suggesting that mastery of metaphor cannot be learned from others, we all use metaphor in our daily language. Practicing the different means of making figurative language is a way to understand its use, bring it into our own writing and speech, and exercise our ability to draw connections in the world. By consciously practicing, we can improve our use of figurative language and become masters of metaphor.

Suggestions for Writing

1. Write about an animal you resemble. I have often thought that people resemble certain animals, either by sheer physical

appearance or by their actions. We all have our bear-like friends, our nervous, hopping sparrows, our darting lizards, languid cats.

2. Compare humans in general to some other animal or plant, in order to make a statement. One student's rather insightful response compared humans to the maleluca, a water-sucking exotic plant originally introduced to help dry up the Everglades but now threatening the entire ecosystem as it spreads swiftly through the region and wipes away native plants. The comparison led into a good discussion about the dangers of introducing exotics into an ecosystem and helped others see the effect humans are having on the world.

3. As in Wilbur's "The Writer," compare the act of writing to something in nature, using an extended metaphor. This kind of exercise also helps us realize how techniques of poetry can be used for more expository purposes.

Symbols, Not Cymbals

Read/Revisit

Richard Wilbur, "The Writer" (see page 218)

Invariably, when we talk about symbols in workshops, someone will ask a question like "Isn't a car ever just a car?" The question recalls Sigmund Freud's famous answer that "sometimes a cigar is just a cigar." Whether something has symbolic value, of course, depends on the context. A car that is used for a getaway, an "accessory" made necessary by the plot, may be just a car, for instance, but your first car usually carries great meaning and symbolism. A symbol asks the reader to ascribe a concept or idea (like freedom) to something tangible (like a car).

Symbols vary from culture to culture, depending on religion, history, landscape, and other elements. However, because they also arise out of our unconscious, there are many similarities between symbols in different cultures. These "universal" symbols or models, such as a flood, a forest, or a fire, are known as archetypes, and they often carry a duality of meaning. A flood is both restorative and destructive, a forest is a place of natural beauty but also danger, and fire gives warmth but has great power to destroy. Symbols often enter one's writing on their own, and only later may the writer realize what has happened on the page. They may carry many layers of meaning.

A piece of writing might be overt about its symbolism, or the symbolism might exist more subtly. An *allegory* is the simplest form of symbolism—a piece in which it is obvious that the elements stand for something. In Nathaniel Hawthorne's well-known story "Young Goodman Brown," for instance, the character named Faith is clearly symbolic. In longer allegorical works such as Dante's *Divine Comedy*, there are often many layers of meaning and interpretation. Because allegory lends itself especially to didactic writing (work that attempts to teach ethical, moral, or religious values), in the wrong hands it can feel like a sledgehammer to the reader. Overt symbols can easily become loud cymbals if the rest of the music is not kept in balance.

We live in an elaborate symbolic matrix. No one can deny it. We can see the evidence on the average drive to work. Deliberately invented symbols in our society such as words, flags, and road signs are usually referred to by scholars as *signs*. We also have *traditional* or *conventional* symbols, such as flowers or religious icons that have a certain meaning in society and that might appear in a writer's work. Writers might also use *private* or *contextual* symbols that develop throughout a single piece (such as the whale in *Moby-Dick*) or ones that recur in different works.

Certain people might take on a legendary or symbolic quality in a culture (Attila the Hun, Socrates, Mother Theresa, Elvis, John F. Kennedy).

Actions are also sometimes symbolic—in real life and on the page. Actions tell a great deal about a person's character.

Wilbur's "The Writer" uses a starling's struggle to escape from a room as a symbol for the experience of a writer. Although he never explicitly declares the symbolism, the connection is very clear, as the speaker watches the bird, trapped in the room, and connects it to his own and his daughter's experience of being a writer.

Suggestions for Writing

1. As in Wilbur's "The Writer," juxtapose two things: an animal and its actions symbolizing a person and his or her actions.

2. In a workshop, look among your possessions for symbolic items. Take out your wallet or purse, for example. What symbolic items do you have in your possession at the moment? Money is a sign for something, of course, but it also functions on a symbolic level. Pictures? A driver's license? Unmentionables? Do you have a piece of jewelry, clothing, or a tattoo that is symbolic? Write a short piece that makes the symbolism of the item clear, but subtle. (You might also use symbolic items in your vicinity—a tree, a blackboard, a painting.)

6
Figurative Language

What you say is important, of course, but *how* you say it often makes the difference. As Robert Frost says, "All the fun's in how you say a thing."

The "how" is made up of a great variety of elements operating simultaneously, some of which have been discussed in other chapters: diction (word choice), syntax (the arrangement of words), figurative language, form. Each of these elements contributes to the *tone* (the stance or attitude) of the piece. Titles might be used to set up the tone from the beginning.

The following is a brief review of types of figurative language, with examples of poetry and prose. Most of the terms derive from the Greek (which gives them their unwieldy quality in English). The techniques, not the terms themselves, are the essential element, although you will probably also learn the terms as you try your hand at them.

> **apostrophe**: addressing something not usually spoken to: an historical figure, a poem, an object, an idea, something in nature.

> O wind, rend open the heat
>
> H.D. (1886–1961)

> Milton! Thou shouldst be living at this hour.
>
> WILLIAM WORDSWORTH (1770–1850)

> **personification**: giving human characteristics to something non-human (an animal, inanimate object, abstract idea, etc.).

> A tattered coat upon a stick, unless
> Soul clap its hands and sing, and louder sing
> For every tatter in its mortal dress
>
> WILLIAM BUTLER YEATS (1865–1939)

> The great crane still swung its black arm from Oxford Street to
> above their heads.
>
> DORIS LESSING (B. 1919)

synesthesia: (from Greek, meaning "blended feeling") the association of an image perceived by one of the senses with one perceived by another.

And taste the music of that vison pale.

JOHN KEATS (1795–1821)

Perfumes there are as sweet as the oboe's sound
Green as prairies, fresh as a child's caress

CHARLES BAUDELAIRE (1821–1867)

hyperbole: (from the Greek, "throwing beyond") exaggeration.

I lost two cities, lovely ones. And, vaster,
some realms I owned, two rivers, a continent.

ELIZABETH BISHOP (1911–1979)

And from far up, ringing from peak to peak of the summits over us, came a cry of such unutterable and ecstatic joy that it sounds down across the years and tingles among the cups of my quiet breakfast table.

LOREN EISELEY (1907–1977)

understatement: something phrased in a restrained way.

. . . for destruction ice
Is also great
And would suffice.

ROBERT FROST (1874–1963)

litotes: (from the Greek, "plain or meager") a type of understatement that makes a point by denying the opposite, such as "He's no angel."

metonymy: referring to something by using the name of something associated with it (e.g., the Church, the Crown, the White House, the silver screen). There are many categories of metonymy, such as using the name of the place for the institution ("Wall Street is jittery"), or the object for the user ("The factories are on strike"). Note how scepter, crown, scythe, and spade represent social classes in the following passage:

Scepter and crown must tumble down
And in the dust be equal made
With the poor crooked scythe and spade.

JAMES SHIRLEY (1596–1666)

synecdoche: (from the Greek, "taking whole") a type of metonymy in which a part refers to the whole.

proud (orgulloso) of his daughter's pen.

RHINA P. ESPAILLAT (B. 1932)

Every day brings a ship,
Every ship brings a word;
Well for those who have no fear,
Looking seaward well assured
That the word the vessel brings
Is the word they wish to hear.

RALPH WALDO EMERSON (1803–1882)

paradox: (from the Greek, meaning "contrary to expectation") a statement that seems like a contradiction but which reveals another layer of truth. Shakespeare's poetry is filled with paradox.

When most I wink, then do mine eyes best see. . . .
All days are nights to see till I see thee.

When my love swears she is made of truth
I do believe her, though I know she lies.

WILLIAM SHAKESPEARE (1564–1616)

Sylvie did not want to lose me. She did not want me to grow gigantic and
    multiple, so that I seemed to fill the whole house.

And below is always the accumulated past, which vanishes but does not
    vanish, which perishes and remains.

MARILYNNE ROBINSON (B. 1944)

oxymoron: compressed paradox, like "jumbo shrimp," or "sweet sorrow."

Parting is such sweet sorrow

WILLIAM SHAKESPEARE (1564–1616)

allusion: reference to another literary work, history, art, event, etc. An allusion might be direct or subtle. Sometimes a work declares an influence directly, such as the quotation from Dante that opens T. S. Eliot's "Love Song of J. Alfred Prufrock." Names are another method of creating allusion, such as Melville's choice of the biblical tyrant Ahab for the captain's name in *Moby-Dick*.

An allusion might also be more subtle, such as the use of a quotation or paraphrase from another author within the piece. Sometimes the allusion has an archetypal quality about it, recalling an age-old story, such as the reference to the Flood in Alice Munro's short story "The Found Boat":

At the end of Bell Street, McKay Street, Mayo Street, there was the Flood. It was the Wawanash River, which every spring overflowed its banks. . . . Light reflected off the water made everything bright and cold, as it is in a lakeside town, and woke or revived in people certain vague hopes of disaster. . . . There were always things floating around in the Flood—branches, fence-rails, logs, road signs, old lumber; sometimes boilers, washtubs, pots and pans, or even a car seat or stuffed chair, as if somewhere the Flood had got into a dump.

ALICE MUNRO (B. 1931)

metaphor: a comparison in which something is directly described as being something else.

Young as she is, the stuff
Of her life is great cargo

RICHARD WILBUR (B. 1921)

She had horses who were bodies of sand.
She had horses who were maps drawn of blood.
She had horses who were skins of ocean water.

JOY HARJO (B. 1951)

extended metaphor: a metaphor that expands on an original comparison. Many poems operate on this principle, as do many prose passages, sometimes extensive works.

In her room a the prow of the house
Where light breaks, and the windows are tossed with linden,
My daughter is writing a story.

I pause in the stairwell, hearing
From her shut door a commotion of typewriter-keys
Like a chain hauled over a gunwhale.

Young as she is, the stuff
of her life is great cargo, and some of it heavy:
I wish her a lucky passage.

RICHARD WILBUR (B. 1921)

simile: a type of metaphor using such words as *like, as, seems, appears*.

And like a thunderbolt he falls.

ALFRED, LORD TENNYSON (1809–1892)

For the letters of my mother's mother
. . . are brown and soft,
And liable to melt as snow

HART CRANE (1899–1932)

implied metaphor: a metaphor that uses neither a connective such as *like* nor a form of the verb *to be*.

In her room, at the prow of the house

RICHARD WILBUR (B. 1921)

There are no stars tonight
But those of memory.

HART CRANE (1899–1932)

In Mississippi I wandered among some of the ghosts and bones, and it is my great lesson to have learned to stop trying to evade and forget what I have seen and heard and understood and now must know, but rather to embrace the ghosts and cradle the bones and call them my own.

ANTHONY WALTON (B. 1960)

analogy: a kind of reasoning (used in the sciences, math, history, and other disciplines) that is based on metaphor and crucial to our process of thinking and making connections. Terry Tempest Williams uses analogy and extended metaphor, as well as other figurative language, in "Peregrine Falcon":

Our urban wastelands are becoming wildlife's last stand. The great frontier. We've moved them out of town like all other low-income tenants. . . . I like to sit on the piles of unbroken Hefties, black bubbles of sanitation. . . . The starlings gorge themselves, bumping into each other like drunks. They are not discretionary. They'll eat anything, just like us. . . . Perhaps we project on to starlings that which we deplore in ourselves: our numbers, our aggression, our greed, and our cruelty. Like starlings, we are taking over the world.

TERRY TEMPEST WILLIAMS (B. 1955)

Writers often use many figures of speech within a single passage, as in the following familiar soliloquy from Shakespeare's *Macbeth* (Act V, Scene 5), which uses nearly all of them.

Tomorrow, and tomorrow, and tomorrow
Creeps in this petty pace from day to day
To the last syllable of recorded time;
And all our yesterdays have lighted fools
The way to dusty death. Out, out, brief candle!
Life's but a walking shadow, a poor player,
That struts and frets his hour upon the stage,
And then is heard no more. It is a tale
Told by an idiot, full of sound and fury,
Signifying nothing.

Suggestions for Writing

1. Look at the passage above from *Macbeth*. How many figures of speech can you identify?

2. A fun way to practice the techniques of figurative language (and simultaneously generate ideas) is to write the terms defined and discussed above on scraps of paper. Now pick three out of a hat. Write a short piece containing all three elements.

3. For a fun but rather challenging exercise, write down several (or all) of the above types of figurative language on scraps of paper. Then write a poem, selecting a different technique at random for each line. "Following orders" in this fashion can help you grasp a particular figure of speech, but the random sequence will also provide you with some unique variations that might not have otherwise arisen—lines or thoughts to use later. In some rare instances, the initial results might actually produce a lasting poem. This exercise often yields rather surreal connections. For instance, use the following devices in the order they are introduced:

line:

one (apostrophe):	Address something nonhuman
two (personification):	Personify something

three (synesthesia):	Use an image mixing sensory perception
four (hyperbole):	Exaggerate
five (understatement/litotes):	Use understatement/Deny the opposite
six (metonymy/synecdoche):	Refer to something by using something related/Use a part for a whole
seven (paradox/oxymoron):	Write a compressed contradiction
eight (allusion):	Allude to something
nine (metaphor):	Use a metaphor
ten (simile):	Extend the metaphor, using simile
eleven (implied metaphor/ analogy):	Extend the metaphor further, using implied metaphor or analogy

4. For a later, much greater challenge using the preceding exercise, you might also incorporate rhyme and meter (see the sections on rhyme and meter in Part Two). The following student response uses nearly all of the above devices in the following order: apostrophe, personification, hyperbole, paradox, synecdoche, allusion, simile, metaphor, extended metaphor.

Valentine

O, my blood, you are so red and busy,
You must get frustrated and want a drink.
So I will fix you hundreds of them, for
Alcohol poisoning might make you think.
Vintage bottles burst forth tiny red cells,
Gentle white ones with the power to kill.
Then, a funeral in my platelets,
Empty as E. Dickinson's windowsill.
You, like the silent chair in which she sat.
I more mischievous, a Cheshire cat,
Her cold fingers stroke my mane . . . life's chess game.

JENNIFER PEARSON, STUDENT

5. In a workshop, the above "following orders" exercise might be done as a collaborative poem with a random quality (the results will likely be even more surreal than the previous exercises).

Each person writes the first line, then passes the paper to the right. Then each person writes the second line and passes the paper, and so on.

Using too much figurative language in a piece of writing, of course, might weigh it down or cause confusion. Some combinations of metaphor might be useful to create a surreal effect, but be wary of creating unintentional *mixed* or *warring* metaphors such as "Language is the river that opens doors" or "The curves on the road unfolded."

7
Diction

Origins of Words

Word choice in English can be particularly daunting, probably because English derives from so many languages. Following is a list of words that derive from Germanic/Anglo-Saxon roots and corresponding words from Greco-Latin roots. Words of Anglo-Saxon origin are often monosyllabic, which makes them particularly useful when writing metrical verse or for achieving the effect of a sparse style.

Germanic/Anglo-Saxon	*Greco-Latin*
house	domicile
woods	forest
dark	obscure
mad	insane
eat	consume
speak	discourse
sorrow	anguish

Suggestions for Writing

1. Write a short piece incorporating only words from the first column. Then rewrite the piece incorporating only words from the second column. Do you notice any difference in the tone?
2. Rewrite the piece in the preceding exercise using words from both columns.

Foreign Flavor

Sometimes the use of a word or words in another language seems essential to conveying aspects of a particular setting. If you grew up with a second language, you may have memories of events that took place in another language. Or you might be writing about a travel experience in a piece that would benefit from the occasional foreign word. The challenge is to let the words add flavor to the rendering in English without overburdening the piece.

Read/Revisit

> Rhina P. Espaillat, "Bilingual/Bilingüe" (poem and essay) (see pages 170 and 174)

Notice how Rhina P. Espaillat uses the register of two languages to write about the conflict of generations. Consider the effect of the parentheses and the reason for the lack of them in the last stanza.

Suggestions for Writing

1. Write a short poem substituting certain words with their equivalent in another language. This probably works best if you are bilingual, but if you are not, you might think of the words you do know in another language. Why do you remember them? Is there a story behind the words or phrases—how they planted themselves in your brain? Use one of these words or phrases as the impetus for a piece. Some words struck me as extraordinarily memorable the first time I heard them, because of their musicality, their root, or their meaning. The Spanish *sueño* feels dreamlike to me. I've always liked the French *plume* because of the feather and pen connection. *Besuchen*, German for visit, contains the word *suchen*, to seek.

2. Write a few lines that include a bit of dialogue between two speakers, one of whom speaks only in English but the other mixes a word or phrase from another language with English. Write the dialogue so the context of the situation and the action of the speakers make it clear what the non-English words mean.

Surrealist Game

Read/Revisit

Lewis Carroll, "Jabberwocky" (see page 165)

Suggestions for Writing

The following exercise derives from a favorite practice of the surrealists, who enjoyed such collaborative, random exercises to produce writing. It was named *Cadavre Exquis* (Exquisite Corpse) allegedly because of a famous line that resulted from it: "The Exquisite Corpse Drinks New Wine." Random though it appears, the exercise is based in the logic of syntax, and it will produce some coherency amidst the random connections.

To do this exercise on your own, you could fill in the blanks as quickly as possible, without giving clear coherency from line to line, and see what results. In a workshop, everyone should begin by filling in the blanks of the first line (try to make the individual line make sense), then pass it to the right. Each person then should write the second line and pass it to the right, and so on. When all the lines are completed, read the results aloud. (For even more surreal results, you could fold the paper to hide each completed line before you pass it.)

> At dawn, the <u>sound adjective, noun type of machine</u>
> began to <u>verb adverb</u>
> next to the <u>color adjective, noun place</u>.
> The <u>smell adjective, noun animal</u>
> <u>verb (past tense) adverb</u>
> on the <u>texture adjective, noun piece of furniture</u>.
> Later that morning, the <u>emotional adjective, noun musical instrument</u>
> <u>verb(past tense) adverb</u>
> through the <u>taste adjective, noun element of landscape</u>.
> This caused the _____.

Example:

> At dawn, the noisy dishwasher
> began to chuckle hysterically
> next to the blue house.
> The rancid cat
> complained loudly
> on the soft couch.
> Later that morning, the sad piano
> howled ferociously
> through the bitter mountains.
> This caused the windows to break.

Simplify

Although some exercises in this chapter suggest ways to use words in fresh, innovative, sometimes surreal arrangements, diction certainly need not be difficult or bizarre to have a powerful effect.

Read/Revisit

> Robert Frost, "The Road Not Taken" (see page 176)
> William Stafford, "Traveling through the Dark" (see page 210)

Consider Frost's well-known poem with new eyes and ears. Read it aloud to appreciate its full impact. The choice of simple but precise words in the poem, such as *diverged, undergrowth, traveler,* and *way*, build the poem's intensity. Frost's poem also builds on a single image. It extends one central metaphor. One of the most evocative lines in the poem is "Yet knowing how way leads on to way"—an inventive syntax that repeats the most simple of words: *way*. Notice, also, how Frost keeps the rhyme fresh by using different parts of speech (noun, adjective, verb, noun, adverb, pronoun, preposition) at the end of each line.

Suggestions for Writing

1. Try emulating Frost's simplicity. Take some cryptic lines from your journal and think about what stories they are concealing. Have the courage to just "tell it straight," as Frost often does. Or write a response to Frost's poem in particular, a conversation with the idea of two roads that forked in your own life.
2. William Stafford's "Traveling through the Dark" uses simple diction and a straightforward manner of narration. Consider the effect of Stafford's choices. Try emulating his style.

Tell-Tale Dialect

Dialect is a difficult element to master in writing, particularly if you are using a dialect with which you are not completely comfortable. Sometimes writers work with linguists or natives of a region to make sure that their characters' speech sounds authentic. The exercise below will get you thinking about the way using a different dialect can entirely change a piece of writing.

Suggestions for Writing

"Translate" a famous passage into a different form of English. This exercise works well as a group activity and provides a good opportunity to talk about the importance of dialect. For instance, use the opening paragraph of Edgar Allan Poe's "The Tell-Tale Heart" and have the murderer use a different dialect (e.g., from the deep South, a Brooklyn youth, Spanglish, etc.).

> True!—nervous—very, very dreadfully nervous I had been and am; but why *will* you say that I am mad? The disease had sharpened my senses— not destroyed—not dulled them. Above all was the sense of hearing acute. I heard all things in the heaven and in the earth. I heard many things in hell. How, then, am I mad? Hearken! and observe how healthily—how calmly I can tell you the whole story.
>
> It is impossible to say how first the idea entered my brain; but, once conceived, it haunted me day and night. Object there was none. Passion there was none. I loved the old man. He had never wronged me. He had never given me insult. For his gold I had no desire. I think it was his eye!—yes, it was this! He had the eye of a vulture—a pale blue eye, with a film over it. Whenever it fell upon me, my blood ran cold; and so, by degrees—very gradually—I made up my mind to take the life of the old man, and thus rid myself of the eye forever.

Example:

> Word!—nervous—I was mad scared, yo! But why you got to be say I'm trippin', you know? The disease woke me up—I ain't sleepin'. My ears was on fire with knowledge! I heard things in da' heaven above and da' earth, and all the way down to Hell. How am I nuts? Peep this! 'Cuz I got a story to tell.
>
> I don't know how it got in my head, yo, but once it was there, yo boom—it haunted me day and night. There was no beef, no hype, 'cuz I had mad love for the old geezer! I ain't got no reason, ain't got no rhyme. He never dissed me. I wasn't trying to take his paper. But he had this nasty ol' lookin' eye. He had eyes like a vulture, blue, all glazed and all! Whenever he peeped me, my blood ran cold, and so over time, I decided to cap him before he got me.
>
> STUDENTS: MICHELLE BYNUM, JEREMY GOLDSMITH, JENNIFER PEARSON

You could, of course, use any of many well-known works for this exercise. The passage is a good, albeit eerie choice because of the urgent voice: the madman who tries to convince us of his sanity. It also contains several archaic words such as *hearken*, which offer opportunity for humorous translations.

8
Drawing Tension

Reversing the Action

Our universe is expanding, with the galaxies speeding away from each other. One of the fundamental questions of cosmology is what the universe's ultimate fate will be. Several theories have been proposed. One of these asserts that the expansion will eventually stop, and the universe will begin to collapse. The physicist Stephen Hawking has suggested that if this theory is correct, the arrows of time will not point in the same direction for the whole history of the cosmos. At the point the universe begins to contract, time as we know it will move backwards.

Martin Amis's book *Time's Arrow* uses Hawking's idea to explore questions of time. He narrates a life story backwards, with a soul trying to make sense of a backwards world. In doing so, he comments satirically about society—from the weighty and grave to the comic and irreverent. The following passage from the novel describes rain, lightning, and earthquakes from a backwards perspective:

> I know I live on a fierce and magical planet, which sheds or surrenders rain or even flings it off in whipstroke after whipstroke, which fires out bolts of electric gold into the firmament at 186,000 miles per second, which with a single shrug of its tectonic plates can erect a city in half an hour. Creation . . . is easy, is quick.

The conversations in the book, too, are backwards:

> "Don't go—please."
> "Goodbye, Tod."
> "Don't go."
> "It's no good."
> "Please."
> "There's no future for us."
> Which I greet, I confess, with a silent "Yeah, yeah." Tod resumes:
> "Elsa," he says, or Rosemary or Juanita or Betty-Jean. "You're very special to me."
> "Like hell."
> "But I love you."
> "I can't look you in the eye."

I have noticed in the past, of course that most conversations would make much better sense if you ran them backward. But with this man-woman stuff, you could run them any way you liked—and still get no further forward.

While recent discoveries provide support for the competing theory that the universe will continue to expand forever, reversing the flow of time in the plot remains a useful literary device. One task for which it is particularly useful is uncovering the true magnitude of events or actions.

W. S. Merwin's piece "Unchopping a Tree" uses the reversal of time to achieve this effect. In the description of the mammals, the nests, the insects that would have to be returned, the splintered trunk reconnected, one senses the enormity of the destruction in the felling of a single tree. In describing the process backwards, he makes a comment about the intricate balance of nature that, once destroyed, is impossible to restore:

> With spiders' webs you must simply do the best you can. We do not have the spider's weaving equipment, nor any substitute for the leaf's living bond with its point of attachment and nourishment.

Suggestions for Writing

Describe something backwards. Create your reverse-time version in order to make a comment about something that has been done that might be better undone (e.g., undevelop a new development, unpollute a river, etc.).

Trading Elements

The mind searches for ways to make sense of disparate elements, to make narrative. Although the following exercise might not always yield the best story, it is a good challenge, and the mere combinations alone often make for good humor (e.g., Napoleon, in class, stage fright; Madonna, Buckingham Palace, UFO sighting).

The combinations that arise can be kernels of later, more substantial pieces.

Suggestions for Writing

1. Have each person write down a character, a place, and an event on three separate scraps of paper. Collect them in piles. Then each participant will select one from each pile. Construct a short narrative using the three elements you have chosen. Try to use each of the elements in an equally significant way. Note the following student example:

   > (a student, a ramshackle cabin, world domination)
   > The school had called a snow day, and Tom had been hunting all day down in the state forest. When he came back to the house, he had no idea where Billy was or what he was up to. He saw the diffuse glow of a single hanging lightbulb coming from the guest cabin located in the far end of the field behind their house. As he brushed through the overgrown reeds in his rubber boots, he saw tiny fireworks bursting sporadically in one of the broken out windows. Billy was doing something with the scraps from the rusted out brick wagon. Tom crept closer. Little glints of light flew, and as Tom felt along the splintery wood walls, it became obvious to him what his brother was doing. The mildewed map of the world was dangling on the wall. The little flags were posted precariously. Billy was at it again.
   >
   > EMILY BUSCH, STUDENT

2. Assign each other titles, based perhaps on heritage and inclinations. The titles might send you where you otherwise would not have gone. Or try a different approach and use titles randomly. In a workshop, come up with titles and then scramble them. Write a piece with the title you receive.

Reverberating Closure

Read/Revisit

> Elizabeth Bishop, "One Art" (see page 161)
> Diane Thiel, "*Memento Mori* in Middle School" (see page 213)
> Nikos Kavadias, "A Knife" (see page 188)
> Edwin Arlington Robinson, "Richard Cory" (see page 205)

Robert Frost says, "Anyone can get into a poem. It takes a poet to get out of one." William Butler Yeats believed good closure occurred when a poem would "come shut with a click, like a closing box." What gives a piece of writing that click? It is hard to identify, but we know it when we see or hear it. Evan Connell's vignettes shut like a door at the end, yet also echo into the next chapter. Perhaps that is the quality closure should have—it should reverberate.

A poignant or startling event, scene, image, or moment can make for good closure. The poem "*Memento Mori* in Middle School," for instance, closes with the image of children yelling after school, showing off "their darkened red and purple tongues."

Closure is sometimes influenced by form. Sonnets, for instance, traditionally closed with a philosophical commentary. And several poetic forms, such as the villanelle, have refrains that often carry a slightly different meaning in the end. A piece might also be left mysterious.

Poems often carry an element of surprise at the end. Dorothy Parker's poems, for instance, are known for their ironic twists, such as one of my favorites, "One Perfect Rose," which is set up as a love poem, with a refrain of "one perfect rose" that the speaker's love always brings. The twist comes in the last stanza, when the speaker wonders why her love has never sent her "one perfect limousine, do you suppose?" Consider, also, the effect of the closure in Edwin Arlington Robinson's "Richard Cory." The end of the poem "makes" the poem, because it is unexpected. The ending works not just because of the element of surprise, but because it reflects accurately the way such events feel when they occur.

Nikos Kavadias's ballad "A Knife" carries a similar element of surprise at the end. We are drawn into the story being narrated by the old dealer, and though filled with the intensity of the violence surrounding the history of the knife, we are still somewhat unprepared for the final line, which continues reverberating after the poem is finished.

There is an old German proverb regarding closure: "Beginning and end shake hands with each other." Sometimes, when we are writing, we know we have reached the end, and it happens naturally, perhaps with an organic, circular structure that contains elements of the opening. Other times we have an idea, but it takes a while to find the right words. And sometimes a piece does not seem to find an end. Try not to force it. It might be telling you to continue down that road.

Suggestions for Writing

1. Try writing a piece with an ironic closure, one that surprises the reader because the opposite of what is expected takes place. Play the trickster. Some real-life stories have a natural irony when they occur, with a clear closure, a line of dialogue, perhaps.

2. Look with new eyes at the closure of a piece you have written. Are there any other ways your piece could end? Write an alternative closure and compare the two. Discussions about closure should be an important aspect of a workshop. Often, as writers, we don't know when to stop; a natural closure might already exist in the piece. Other sets of eyes can help identify what is missing or what can be cut.

9
Sound and Rhythm

Listening to Nature

Read/Revisit

William Butler Yeats, "The Lake Isle of Innisfree" (see page 225)

The natural world is filled with songs. We can learn a great deal about the rhythms of nature by just listening. Go to the ocean, a waterfall, a river near your home. Listen for a while. Then try writing as you listen. How does it affect your rhythm?

Go into the woods and listen to the trees. Listen to the wind in the trees. Stay very still and listen to bird calls for a while. Then write. What might they be saying? Can you tell the tone of their songs? Do you hear the scolding shriek of a bluejay, the wild laugh of a loon, or the lyrical song of a warbler? Do they sound like anything you know?

You might also be able to discern certain rhythms with your eyes. A good example is a lizard's dewlap. I have sat mesmerized by the hypnotic beat of the dewlap concealed in the throat, revealing itself again and again.

Think about your own voice. What physical realities make the sounds and words emerge? Why do people from different regions have different accents? Do we train our mouths to move in a certain way? In a favorite novel of mine, David Malouf's *An Imaginary Life*, there is a passage where the Roman poet Ovid is teaching a wild boy to speak. The boy can imitate all the birds and animals of the woods, but rather than merely mimicking, he seems to become the creature:

> His whole face is contorted differently as he assumes each creature's voice. If he were to speak always as frog or hawk or wolf, the muscles of his throat and jaw might grow to fit the sound, so intimately are the creatures and the sounds they make connected, so deeply are they one. . . . I have begun to understand him. In imitating the birds, he is not, like our mimics, copying something that is outside him and revealing the accuracy of his ear or the virtuosity of his speech organs. He is being the bird. He is allowing it to speak out of him.

Try making the sounds you hear. What new muscles do you use? One interesting and easy exercise to do in the wild will attract many birds to you. Conceal yourself well and make repeated *psh psh psh* sounds. The sounds imitate the scolding calls of many birds. It can also be a meditative experience to remain still and call like that. Listen to the responses you get. Are there rhythms, repetitions? Imagine yourself as an arriving bird. What are you hearing? What are you thinking as you respond?

In Malouf's book, as Ovid learns more about the wild boy, he realizes how deeply the boy is connected to the universe. If he is to understand the child, he needs to "think as he must: I am raining. I am thundering."

Suggestions for Writing

1. Imitate the rhythm of a sound you hear—a bird call, the ocean. Let your form reflect something in the natural world. Robinson Jeffers's long lines, for instance, reflect the rhythm of the dramatic Pacific tides.

2. You might also listen for the rhythms of something other than the natural world. Let the rhythms of everyday speech find their way into your writing. You might also try to capture the pace of a city—the positives or the negatives.

3. In "Ode to a Nightingale," John Keats reflects on the unchanging music of the nightingale throughout history:

> Perhaps the selfsame song that found a path
> Through the sad heart of Ruth, when, sick for home,
> She stood in tears amid the alien corn;
> The same that oft-times hath
> Charmed magic casements, opening on the foam
> Of perilous seas, in faery lands forlorn.
>
> JOHN KEATS (1795–1821)

Let the music in nature take you to another realm. Write about another era in which this song was heard.

4. Some words seem to have sounds as their origin—crunch, growl, splash, hum—an effect known as *onomatopoeia*, from the Greek, meaning "name-making." A sophisticated use of onomatopoeia can be heard in the following well-known lines by Alfred, Lord Tennyson:

> The moan of doves in immemorial elms,
> And murmuring of innumerable bees.
>
> ALFRED, LORD TENNYSON (1809–1892)

As you listen to sounds around you, repeat the sounds, listening to your own voice for the words they bring to mind. Keep a list of such words. Incorporate them in a piece of writing.

Finding Your Rhythm:
Poetry in Prose

Rhythm is an organic part of our everyday lives—in the tides, crickets in the night, our heartbeats. What makes rhythm in a piece of writing? Rhythm is defined as a systematic variation in the flow of sound. In poetry, rhythm might be regular, via the use of meter (discussed in Part Two). Or it might be based on the unit of breath. The repetition of key words and phrases is a technique of free verse and the prose poem. (Rhythm in poetry is discussed extensively in the "Rhythm and Refrain" and "Hearing the Beat: Using Meter" chapters in Part Two.) But there is much that good prose can learn from poetic technique as well.

Consider the following passage from Marilynne Robinson's novel *Housekeeping*:

> Looking out at the lake one could believe that the Flood had never ended. If one is lost on the water, any hill is Ararat. And below is always the accumulated past, which vanishes but does not vanish, which perishes and remains. If we imagine that Noah's wife when she was old found somewhere a remnant of the Deluge, she might have walked into it till her widow's dress floated above her head and the water loosened her plaited hair. And she would have left it to her sons to tell the tedious tale of generations. She was a nameless woman, and so at home among all those who were never found and never missed, who were uncommemorated, whose deaths were not remarked, nor their begettings.

Robinson's choice of language is a beautiful example of poetry within prose. If you read the above passage aloud, you will notice the rhythm of the sentences, the near iambic lines such as "If one is lost on the water, any hill is Ararat," "If we imagine that Noah's wife when she was old," or "whose deaths were not remarked, nor their begettings." She even uses internal assonance (such as *past* and *vanish*, or *tale* and *hair*) and alliteration (such as *tedious tale*). There are parallel structures such as "which vanishes but does not vanish, which perishes and remains" and "who were never found and never missed, who were uncommemorated, whose deaths were not remarked." Notice also the variation of sentence length and structure. Much of the music of this type of passage is best heard, however, when read aloud.

President Lincoln, in his Gettysburg Address, employed poetic techniques so effectively that the speech has been often called a poem, and it is one of the very few speeches (and perhaps the only presidential address) to be considered a piece of literature. Phrases such as "we cannot dedicate—we cannot consecrate—we cannot hallow this ground" employ repetition and variation to full rhythmical effect. Certain portions of the speech even employ meter: "The world will little note nor long remember what we say" is in perfect iambs.

> Four score and seven years ago our fathers brought forth upon this continent a new nation conceived in Liberty, and dedicated to the proposition that all men are created equal.
>
> Now we are engaged in a great civil war, testing whether that nation or any nation so conceived and so dedicated can long endure. We are met on a great battlefield of that war. We are met to dedicate a portion of it as the final resting place of those who here gave their lives that that nation might live. It is altogether fitting and proper that we should do this.
>
> But in a larger sense we cannot dedicate—we cannot consecrate—we cannot hallow this ground. The brave men living and dead who struggled here have consecrated it far above our poor power to add or detract. The world will little note nor long remember what we say here, but it can never forget what they did here. It is for us, the living, rather to be dedicated here to the unfinished work that they have thus far so nobly carried on. It is rather for us to be here dedicated to the great task remaining before us—that from these honored dead we take increased devotion to that cause for which they here gave the last full measure of devotion—that we here highly resolve that the dead shall not have died in vain—that the nation shall, under God, have a new birth of freedom—and that governments of the people, by the people, and for the people, shall not perish from the earth.

Suggestions for Writing

1. Try to discover what your natural rhythm might be. Take a passage of your writing and study various elements. For instance, what is the ratio of short to long sentences? What repetition of sentence structure do you see? Do you notice repetitions of words?

2. Take a favorite passage of prose that has an evocative rhythm. Look at it closely and examine what elements contribute to that rhythm. What poetic techniques can you identify in the passage?

Sound, Sense, and Nonsense

Read/Revisit

Lewis Carroll, "Jabberwocky" (see page 165)

A twelve-year-old girl gave me the idea for the following exercise. She had written about the hoppergrass, the name she had given the grasshopper. That day, we flipped words around. We made a list of some of the words, which we read together as a single poem:

Hoppergrass
lifewild
flybutter
grownover
fedunder
lesschild
lesscare
grass-saw
dozerbull
centershopping
stormthunder
fallrain
flyfire
lightmoon
lifewild
gladesever

Turning each word around gave it a new kind of resonance. e.e. cummings loved wordplay and the sounds of words. "Anyone Lived in a Pretty How Town" is one of my favorites. It is a nature poem, a love poem, a poem about the existential experience, a poem carried by sound. It is a poem that opens up further by discussion.

When I first came across the lines "he sang his didn't he danced his did," somehow, I knew instinctively this was a philosophy of life I wanted to follow.

It can be useful to try opening the language in poetry like e.e. cummings's, or in prose like James Joyce's. At this point, though, you might not want to sustain it for as long as, say, Joyce's 628 pages of Finnegan's Wake, which begins:

riverrun, past Eve and Adam's, from swerve of shore to bend of bay, brings us by a commodius vicus of recirculation back to Howth Castle and Environs.

Sir Tristram, violer d'amores, fr'over the short sea, had passencore rearrived from North Armorica on this side the scraggy isthmus of Europe Minor to wielderfight his penisolate war: nor had topsawyer's rocks by the stream Oconee exaggerated themselse to Laurens County's gorgios while they went doublin their mumper all the time: nor avoice from afire bellowed mishe mishe to tauftauf thuartpeatrick: not yet, though venissoon after, had a kidscad buttended a bland old isaac: not yet, though all's fair in vanessy, were sosie sesthers wroth with twone nathandjoe. Rot a peck of pa's malt had Jhem or Shen brewed by arclight and rory end to the regginbrow was to be seen ringsome on the aquaface.

The fall (bababadalgharaghtakamminarronnkonnbronnton-nerronntuonnthunntrovarrhounawnskawntoohoohoordenenthurnuk!) of a once wallstraight oldparr is retaled early in bed and later on life down through all christian minstrelsy.

After *Finnegan's Wake*, Lewis Carroll's "Jabberwocky" seems like plain English. Despite Carroll's many made-up words, the events of the story are clear, possibly because of the archetypal pattern of the slaying of a dragon, the conflict of David and Goliath.

Suggestions for Writing

1. Make a list of compound words that could be grouped under one subject. Flip the words, as in "Hoppergrass." Make a list poem.

2. Choose one of the words you created in the preceding exercise and use it as a point from which to leap. Call your piece "Gladesever," for instance.

3. Mix up the parts of speech. Let verbs become nouns and nouns become adjectives. Let yourself be carried by the language. You can worry later about what it means.

4. Imitate "Jabberwocky." Give it a contemporary flair. Write about an encounter with a physical or metaphysical "jabberwocky" of your own. Notice the meter and rhyme scheme that give the poem its shape and sound. Try to imitate this aspect as well: iambic tetrameter, with iambic trimeter in the last line of each stanza, and a rhyme scheme of abab (see "Hearing the Beat: Using Meter" in Part Two).

5. I read *Finnegan's Wake* in a reading group with many Joyce scholars and the help of a published skeleton key. But a first approach to Joyce's style might be to see how much sense can be gleaned from the sound. Read each sentence in the above passage aloud, and then paraphrase it without too much thought. In a workshop, it is fun to see the many different interpretations that result.

10
Speaker and Dialogue

Inhabitation

Read/Revisit

Robert Browning, "My Last Duchess" (see page 162)

Robert Frost once wrote, "When I say me in a poem, it's someone else. / When I say somebody else, it might be me." Sometimes writing with a different voice allows us to explore aspects about ourselves we might not otherwise reveal. Sometimes it allows us to come closer to someone else's experience. Try inhabiting one of the characters in a story (with whom you identify perhaps) and write from the *persona* you create. You could give someone a voice who previously had none. You might, for instance, inhabit an animal from a myth or fairy tale.

Victorian poet Robert Browning (1812–1889) developed the form of the *dramatic monologue* (a speech that creates a dramatic scene) in a poem. He often used the form to explore the psyches of weak, troubled, or crazy characters. His "My Last Duchess," likely the most famous dramatic monologue ever written, takes on the voice of an Italian Renaissance duke:

> She thanked men, —good! but thanked
> Somehow—I know not how—as if she ranked
> My gift of a nine-hundred-years-old name
> With anybody's gift.

The narrator of David Malouf's novel *An Imaginary Life* assumes the voice of the Roman poet Ovid, who is exiled to a region where no one can speak his language. It is this element of the story that Malouf enters most fully:

> I have come to a decision. The language I shall teach the Child is the language of these people I have come among, and not after all my own. And in making that decision I know I have made another. I shall never go back to Rome. . . . More and more in these last weeks I have come to realize that this place is the true destination I have been seeking.

Suggestions for Writing

1. Make a list of historical or mythological figures you would like to "inhabit." Consider the particular aspect of their lives that intrigues you. You might need to do some research in order to have your facts straight. Try a dramatic monologue from one of your chosen perspectives, focusing on a particular "story" of the figure's life. You may be surprised how the voice comes when you call it, as in the following student example:

> (Inhabitation of Federico Garcia Lorca)
> People think that being a poet means that every minute there's a poem in your head, that every time of silence, there are little mechanisms in your creative fiber that produce stanzas and lines of love and pain, the only two emotions that are valuable. But it's not that simple. It's not like jumping into a pool and coming out with all sorts of ideas and dreams and stories. Sometimes a poem is written in blood—it comes to you in pain and agony. Sometimes it is like sweet nectar so soothing to the palate. . . . Poetry is fire and ice, my friend.
>
> JORGE FERNANDEZ, STUDENT

2. Inhabit an animal, or an inanimate object, or natural phenomenon, like a hurricane.

3. Repeat the preceding exercise as a group project, one that will emphasize the web of connections. Each person might choose to be a different voice of a certain ecosystem. I have done this exercise with groups of college students as well as young kids. A group of middle school students made a skit out of the voices, called "The Everglades Council," with the council being made up of various members of the ecosystem. I was pleased to see that students chose to be the tiny things as well as the large: the apple snail and the snail kite, as well as the alligator. Some students chose to be the voice of the sun, the water, the wind. One chose to be the human.

4. In another variation of the preceding exercises, write through the voice, but make it a riddle of sorts, never directly stating what you are. This is a useful exercise to see if your description is effective.

Populating a Piece

Read/Revisit

Nikos Kavadias, "A Knife" (see page 188)

Just as the real world is populated by living things, literature is populated by characters. The term "living things" is used here deliberately, to emphasize that nonhuman characters figure prominently in many important pieces of literature—especially certain forms such as children's literature, fairy tales, myths, science fiction, and nature writing.

Characters in literature can be described via a number of literary devices. While some of these devices may be specific to a genre, there are three that are common to all four genres: description, dialogue (direct or indirect), and thoughts. The process of presenting a character is called *characterization*.

Characters can be presented in varying detail or *depth*. When little detail is provided, the character is superficial or two-dimensional—*flat*. When the characterization provides more details, the character is more realistic or three-dimensional. Typically, it is the secondary characters in a piece that are flat, but there are important exceptions. The lack of depth in characterization tends to produce characters that are stereotypes, such as the tall, dark, handsome lover, or the ugly, crude villain. Consequently, flat characterization of main characters is particularly appropriate for parody, allegory, or a lighter piece that is intended purely to amuse.

Suggestions for Writing

1. Describe an interesting stranger you came across in the street (or the park, airport, etc.). Focus your description exclusively on appearance and what it conveys about the character.

2. Create a nonhuman character and a human character and write a story or a poem about a special relationship that develops between them. Endow the nonhuman character with human characteristics and imagine a fantastic relationship, one that can never happen in reality.

Dropping from the Eaves

We all have a natural curiosity about other people's lives. If we didn't, story-telling would have no place in our world. Tuning in to other people's lives, particularly in places where we are anonymous, can offer inspiration. Of course, many people today eavesdrop in chatrooms on the Internet, which can be an interesting experience in itself. But people don't tend to tell elaborate stories on the Internet, and there is something about the *overheard* story that can give a richness and reality to your listening, and later to your writing.

Eavesdropping—the word itself is like a poem, like the words dropping magically from the eaves into your own writing.

Suggestions for Writing

1. Here is your license to eavesdrop. Go to a public space (a café, the beach, a bus, a train, any place where you might mingle with people from many walks of life). Give yourself different "listening" exercises. Try to catch some dialogue, intonation. Transcribe the actual words people say. (But be as discreet as possible. People tend to sense an ear bending toward them to hear better.)

   > Hallelujahs mask oh-no-she-didn'ts. . . .
   > She didn't invite *who* to the wedding?
   > Guess who's not invited to the mother's banquet.
   > Deacon Wiley's sleeping with *who*?
   > No wonder she hasn't been to choir practice. . . .
   > Sister Jones is testifying once again
   > Going on about how the Lord brought her a Lexus.
   >
   > MICHELLE BYNUM, STUDENT

2. Use the eavesdropping to create a *dramatic monologue*. Let the character's speech create a dramatic scene.

11
Conversations between Texts

Making the Old Story New

Read/Revisit

W. H. Auden, "Musée des Beaux Arts" (see page 160)
R. S. Gwynn, "Shakespearean Sonnet" (see page 181)
Diane Thiel, "*Memento Mori* in Middle School" (see page 213)

Our stories never change. They simply take on different forms. Once we learn to recognize archetypes (patterns or models present in the unconscious as well as in our heritage of art), we can often see them at work in sources as varied as fairy tales, nursery rhymes, ancient myths, contemporary stories, and in our own writing.

There are countless sources available today that show how archetypes can be used to understand various aspects of our lives—from psychology, to relationships, to job-related issues. The works of psychologist Carl Jung and mythologist Northrop Frye are classic sources. A rather accessible source as an introduction to archetype is Joseph Campbell. His *Hero with a Thousand Faces* draws on the idea of the same stories existing in different cultures, with the heroes and dragons wearing different faces but undergoing similar journeys, trials, and revelations. ("The Hero's Adventure," in particular, in a series of videotaped interviews with Campbell called *The Power of Myth* provides an excellent introduction.)

Of course, there can be a danger in being too aware of archetypes as we recreate them. And one can say this about any kind of art—that, on some level, it is good not to be too aware. Sometimes, the first conscious efforts at using myth or archetype can yield rather clunky results. Nonetheless, it is good practice to let the mind connect story to story, to become familiar with recurring themes, symbols, and sequences of action: the battle, the cycle of life, the forest, the flood, the fountain, the journey. Then they will begin to wander your writing with more fluidity.

All works of art can be explored for archetypal ideas. Certain works have become patterns after which many other pieces are modeled. Some works declare the influence of such a text in the very title: James Joyce's *Ulysses* or Derek Walcott's *The Odyssey* or *Homeros*, for example, establish the connection with Homer's *Odyssey* and the archetype of the journey.

Many writers use other works of literature, from ancient texts to fairy tales, as explicit points of departure. They might use means such as exploring a particular character or sequence of action, or add an ironic twist or ending. American humorist James Thurber retells the story of "Little Red Riding Hood," a classic example of the archetypal encounter in the dark forest. Thurber's version, however, ends with the girl pulling a revolver out of her basket and shooting the wolf dead. The moral that ends the parody is: "Little girls aren't as foolish as they used to be."

Sometimes a writer will choose to write from the point of view of a character who doesn't have much of a voice in the original work. John Gardner's novel *Grendel*, for instance, tells the story of Beowulf from the perspective of the monster, Grendel. Likewise, Jean Rhys's novel *Wide Sargasso Sea* tells the story of Rochester's insane first wife, who has no voice in Charlotte Bronte's *Jane Eyre*.

R. S. Gwynn's "Shakespearean Sonnet" uses the form of a Shakespearean sonnet to reflect on fourteen plays in fourteen lines. Gwynn received the inspiration for the poem from a blurb in an issue of *TV Guide* that reduced *Hamlet* to the unintentionally iambic line: "A man is haunted by his father's ghost." The compression of each of the plays supplies much of the humor in the poem.

The poem "*Memento Mori* in Middle School" recounts a childhood project about Dante's *Inferno*. The poem uses a middle school setting to explore a journey on many levels. Dante himself, in his epic, used the classic archetype of the journey and descent into the dark. The poem offers an interesting example of subject finding form—a loosely rhymed terza rima in homage to Dante. Note the variation of different types of rhyme: exact, slant, assonantal. (See "Committing a Rhyme" in Part Two.)

Suggestions for Writing

1. Choose a myth, fairy tale, or other well-known story, and use the general motif or plot to reflect on something or narrate a story (perhaps make it contemporary). You might also change the tale somewhat for comic purposes, as in James Thurber's version of "Little Red Riding Hood," mentioned above. There are numerous models to follow, several of which are included in this book. A few suggestions: Auden's poem "Musée des Beaux Arts," Yeats's poem "Leda and the Swan," Anne Sexton's poems in her collection *Transformations*, Ursula Le Guin's story "The Wife's Story." If you like, the symbols or patterns of action in the fairy tale or myth

might provide more subtle undercurrents for your piece, rather than a retelling (Alice Munro's story "The Found Boat" and Joyce Carol Oates's story "Where Are You Going, Where Have You Been" are a few examples you might use as inspiration).

2. Find folk tales or myths from different cultures: Native American, African, Chinese, etc. Note any connections to stories with which you are familiar. Write a piece that explores an archetypal theme or symbol in the stories: creation, a flood, transformation, etc. Perhaps use a line from the tale as an epigraph. (Your response might have a contemporary slant. For instance, write about a flood in your hometown.)

3. Respond to a well-known work of literature, perhaps by taking on a character's voice (perhaps one who doesn't have much of a voice in the original).

4. Respond to a work of art, emulating the shape and progression of the piece, as in "*Memento Mori* in Middle School," which, in a tongue-in-cheek manner, uses the archetype of the journey (moving, instead of through the circles of Hell, from red posterboard to red posterboard in a middle school project) and unites the trials of the *Inferno* with a trial-filled middle school experience.

5. Use a form for a distinct purpose of responding to a text. R. S. Gwynn writes his one-line compressions of Shakespeare's plays as a Shakespearean sonnet. "*Memento Mori* in Middle School" responds to Dante by using a variation of Dante's terza rima. Respond to a well-known piece, using the form of the piece to do so.

6. The most well-known poems can be excellent choices for *parody* (an imitation of a work, or a writer's style, often mocking, for humorous purposes). For instance, try writing a parody of Frost's "The Road Not Taken." Maybe use two roads that "diverge" in your hometown (e.g., one goes to school, the other to the bar).

Song and Story

Read/Revisit

William Butler Yeats, "The Stolen Child" (see page 223)
Michael S. Harper, "Dear John, Dear Coltrane" (see page 185)
Edwin Arlington Robinson, "Richard Cory" (see page 205)
Paul Simon, "Richard Cory" (see page 208)

Music, of course, is a great source of inspiration and has been closely linked to literature throughout ages and cultures, as in the traditional ballads of Ireland or the operas and ballets that have set many great works of literature to music. In the oral tradition of ancient Greece, poetry was often set to music. The choruses of tragedies and comedies were sung, with or without instrumental music. This tradition in Greece continues to this day. A great many contemporary Greek musicians set famous ancient and modern poems to music. Many composers elsewhere do the same, though not to the same degree, perhaps.

We can explore different angles on works of literature via contemporary versions, such as Greg Brown's rendition of Blake's *Songs of Innocence and Experience* or Loreena McKennitt's renditions of folk songs and poems such as Yeats's "The Stolen Child."

Many contemporary musicians allude to works of literature. Dire Straits has an interesting "Romeo and Juliet," which gives the old story contemporary language, such as "juliet the dice were loaded from the start."

Paul Simon adopts Edwin Arlington Robinson's "Richard Cory" for his 1960s song, which uses the same title. Simon chooses a different form for his song, a ballad. (See "Ballad and Ballade" in Part Two.) He also makes a number of changes in diction and pronouns, using the first person instead of the third. Consider the purpose of these changes.

Many twentieth-century songs use traditional forms, such as the ballads of Woody Guthrie and Bob Dylan. Dylan's "Boots of Spanish Leather" is particularly powerful because of its poignant closure and its intriguing dialogue. The song tells the story of someone going off to sea. It is sung in two voices, and in Dylan's original, it appears that the man is being left behind and the woman is going off to sea. But in numerous renditions by other artists, the woman is left behind, and the man is heading off to sea. This possibility of performing the lyric either way makes it particularly intriguing. The leaver asks several times what gift might be desired, but repeatedly, the one being left behind just asks for the leaver to come back "unspoiled."

When the one at home gets a letter from the one at sea, which states the uncertainty of return, "depending on how I'm feeling," the one left behind knows the score and in graceful, but practical resignation, finally agrees to accept a gift and asks for boots of Spanish leather.

Song, story, and poetry are linked in the form of the ballad, which offers a good sense of the lineage in music. Tracing the influences on contemporary music can be an enlightening process: rock and roll emerged, for instance, out of rhythm and blues. (See "Blues Poetry" in Part Two.)

Songs may be where people go to find their poetry, perhaps because of the artificial distinctions between poetry and song in our culture. In truth, the two are more linked than it would sometimes appear.

Suggestions for Writing

1. Listen to poems you know that have been set to music. See what emerges beneath your pen during or after. Do you feel differently about the poem after you hear it sung?

2. Listen to your favorite song (rock, rap, country, hip-hop, etc.) with the intention of free-writing afterwards. Use the song as a leaping-off point. Perhaps use a line as an epigraph.

3. Imitate the rhythm of different kinds of music with your lines or sentences. Let the rhythm of your lines or sentences reflect the influence of the beat.

4. Listen to songs in a language you don't know. Can you tell the tone of the song—longing, joy, reverence? "Translate" the song via the tone.

5. Listen to classical music. Try writing as you listen. Try Beethoven's Sixth Symphony, particularly the "Storm Passage" created by violins and cellos. (If you introduce it to others who do not know the piece, you might withhold the name at first, to see what kind of "stormy" feelings get evoked and appear beneath the pen.)

6. Loreena McKennitt may have chosen to set "The Stolen Child" to music because of the refrain, which made it a natural candidate. Try writing a poem with a refrain.

7. Michael S. Harper's "Dear John, Dear Coltrane" responds to a tragedy via a jazz-influenced style. How does the form of the poem contribute to its impact?

8. Choose a poem from a different era and write a new version of it, as Paul Simon did in "Richard Cory."

"Kubla Khan" Continued

"Kubla Khan" is Samuel Taylor Coleridge's famous fifty-four-line fragment. In a prefatory note to the poem, Coleridge explains that an entire poem (200–300 lines) appeared to him in a dream. In ill health, he had fallen asleep after taking a painkiller (probably laudanum). He was reading *Purchas His Pilgrimage*, most likely the following sentences: "Here the Kubla Khan commanded a palace to be built, and a stately garden thereunto. And thus ten miles of fertile ground were inclosed with a wall." Coleridge believed he composed the entire poem in his sleep but adds: "if that indeed can be called composition in which all the images rose up before him as *things*, with a parallel production of the correspondent expressions, without any sensation or consciousness of effort." On waking, he began to write down what he remembered. He was interrupted, however, by a person on business who took him away from the poem for more than an hour. When he returned to his room, Coleridge found that the rest of the poem had escaped his memory. This account, however, has often been considered a fictitious story that Coleridge created about the poem.

Like other Romantics, Coleridge believed writing to be an "organic" rather than a mechanical act. He rejected the notion of a work of art as being "mechanically" contrived to please a certain audience, for instance. He spoke of art as a living entity, growing and developing as one. This philosophy may have had something to do with his refusal to finish the fragment, which he felt had come to an unfortunate, untimely end. Or the fragment may, indeed, have been a fiction, meant to represent the subconscious and the organic nature of art. Because conflicting accounts from Coleridge himself exist, the circumstances surrounding the poem remain somewhat mysterious.

One can certainly relate to the notion of the interrupted process or idea, though our accounts may not be as dramatic as Coleridge's loss of 200 composed lines. Many poets have since attempted to complete the famous fragment, reproduced below. (The Khan is a reference to the first khan, or ruler of the Mongol dynasty in thirteenth-century China. The named places are fictitious, as is the topography.)

Kubla Khan

Or a Vision in a Dream. A Fragment

In Xanadu did Kubla Khan
A stately pleasure dome decree:
Where Alph, the sacred river, ran
Through caverns measureless to man
  Down to a sunless sea.
So twice five miles of fertile ground

With walls and towers were girdled round:
And there were gardens bright with sinuous rills,
Where blossomed many an incense-bearing tree;
And here were forests ancient as the hills,
Enfolding sunny spots of greenery.

But oh! that deep romantic chasm which slanted
Down the green hill athwart a cedarn cover!
A savage place! as holy and enchanted
As e'er beneath a waning moon was haunted
By woman wailing for her demon lover!
And from this chasm, with ceaseless turmoil seething,
As if this earth in fast thick pants were breathing,
A mighty fountain momently was forced:
Amid whose swift half-intermitted burst
Huge fragments vaulted like rebounding hail,
Or chaffy grain beneath the thresher's flail:
And 'mid these dancing rocks at once and ever
It flung up momently the sacred river.
Five miles meandering with a mazy motion
Through wood and dale the sacred river ran,
Then reached the caverns measureless to man,
And sank in tumult to a lifeless ocean:
And 'mid this tumult Kubla heard from far
Ancestral voices prophesying war!

    The shadow of the dome of pleasure
    Floated midway on the waves;
    Where was heard the mingled measure
    From the fountains and the caves.
It was a miracle of rare device,
A sunny pleasure dome with caves of ice!

    A damsel with a dulcimer
    In a vision once I saw:
    It was an Abyssinian maid,
    And on her dulcimer she played,
    Singing of Mount Abora.
    Could I revive within me
    Her symphony and song,
    To such a deep delight 'twould win me
That with music loud and long
I would build that dome in air,
That sunny dome! those caves of ice!
And all who heard should see them there.
And all should cry Beware! Beware!
His flashing eyes, his floating hair!

Weave a circle round him thrice,
And close your eyes with holy dread,
For he on honey-dew hath fed,
And drunk the milk of Paradise.

SAMUEL TAYLOR COLERIDGE (1772–1834)

Suggestions for Writing

Though you might endeavor to complete the poem on your own, you could also try writing a collaborative closure.

In a group, read the poem aloud. Notice how Coleridge uses rhyme, though not in a recurring pattern. The poem also has a generally iambic beat. Sometimes the line has five beats, sometimes four. (See "Hearing the Beat: Using Meter" in Part Two.)

After noting such elements, read the poem aloud again, to get back into the rhythm. Each person should then write the next line of the poem, keeping in mind the general iambic beat and changing rhyme scheme. Don't give the meaning of the line too much thought, but allow the unconscious to take over somewhat. Try to "catch" the rhythm. Take only a minute or two per line. Then pass the papers to the right.

Feel free to go with your first thoughts, however odd. One participant, after Coleridge's lines "For he on honey-dew hath fed, / And drunk the milk of paradise," began with the line "And then, he ate a cantaloupe."

Each person then writes a second line and passes the paper. This continues until the papers have traveled around the room, and you have the one with which you began. Complete the poem with your own final line. Read a few of the completing lines aloud.

12
Performing the Poem: Reading, Slam, Performance

Read/Revisit

Dudley Randall, "Ballad of Birmingham" (see page 204)
Nikos Kavadias, "A Knife" (see page 188)

Poetry is a genre particularly conducive to performance. In their earliest incarnations, poems were, of course, intended to be performed. The stories and history of cultures were passed down in poetry via meter and rhyme, useful as tools to enhance our memory. When we speak of the oral tradition, we often think of times as distant as ancient Greece, of Homeric songs carried from one place to another by memory. Modern Greece, however, is a good example of a place where the oral tradition has survived—perhaps because for many centuries Greece was under foreign rule. Writing could be censored, but no one could suppress or confiscate songs.

Learning poems by heart is a way to honor our oral traditions. As a child, did you learn any poems by heart? Think of what the words suggest: "by heart." We enter a poem more fully when we make it part of our memory. We claim it as our own.

Suggestions for Performance

1. In a workshop, have everyone in your group share a favorite poem. In your recitations, try to inhabit the poem as fully as possible with your voice. Later, share a poem you have written yourself and have committed to memory.

2. Choose a poem that has more than one voice, such as Nikos Kavadias's "A Knife" or Dudley Randall's "Ballad of Birmingham." Choose a partner and practice a performance of the poem. Commit your lines to memory. In a group, you might also have two sets of people perform the same poem, in order to see how different interpretations of the poem might change the presentation.

3. Select a poem in translation and perform the poem with a partner, having one person recite the English version and the other person recite the poem in the original language.

4. Select a poem that does not necessarily have more than one voice. With a partner, figure out an inventive way to share the lines. Then perform the poem.

5. Be creative and figure out an inventive way to dramatize a poem, either by yourself or with a partner. You could use props, music, dramatic gestures, etc.

6. Have a class "slam." Choose three judges. Each of the remaining students will perform a poem. Or, if a poem lends itself to more than one voice, you may break up in groups of two or three and perform one together.

13
Revision

Rereading, Reimagining, Reshaping

So, you have finished the first draft of your piece. Reward yourself with something, and get ready for the next stage of writing: revising.

Begin by rereading your piece. Be critical. Evaluate the parts as well as the whole. Try asking yourself why anyone would want to read this piece—what is its meaning and purpose. A writer rarely begins a piece knowing what its meaning will be; even when he or she does, the intended meaning will change in the process of writing. In creative writing, meaning and purpose emerge organically, as the piece is shaped. As Joan Didion said, "I write to find out what I'm thinking." Meaning and purpose become clearer as the piece is finished. Identifying and articulating them can be an iterative process that helps you reimagine, reorganize, and reshape your piece until it is finished.

Suggestions for Rewriting

1. Read your piece carefully, slowly. Then write down what is at stake in it, what its meaning and purpose are. The longer your answer, the more likely the stakes are not well defined and not high enough. Pare down your answer to one or two sentences. Make sure that what is at stake is compelling enough. If the meaning and purpose of your piece are not very compelling, restate them so they are.

2. Reimagine your piece. What do you need to change in it—what scenes, images, statements do you need to delete, insert, or revise—to achieve the revised meaning and purpose?

3. Repeat the process described above until you can describe the central idea of your piece in a single short, concise sentence. Now reduce the meaning of this sentence to a short list of words (as few as one and no more than five). Express each word in your list in an image, a statement, or a short dialogue. Insert these in your piece and read it again. Does the added material strengthen your piece? Does it clarify the piece's meaning and purpose?

Drafts and Discovery

Read/Revisit

Elizabeth Bishop, "One Art" (see page 161)
Wendy Cope, "Lonely Hearts" (see page 167)

Elizabeth Bishop provides a wonderful example of the importance of revision in writing a poem. It is extraordinarily useful to examine a writer's drafts of a particular piece, both to understand his or her progress and to help develop your own. Bishop left quite a paper trail and is known for spending decades to complete some of her poems. Her famous "The Moose," for instance, took about twenty years to complete. Her villanelle "One Art," Bishop has declared, was surprisingly easy, "like writing a letter." Yet seventeen drafts exist of the poem. For Bishop, seventeen drafts was an *easy* process.

"One Art" is a great example of what can happen in the process of revision and the discoveries that can be made in the process of developing an idea. Brett C. Millier writes:

> Elizabeth Bishop left seventeen drafts of her poem "One Art" among her papers. In the first draft, she lists all the things she's lost in her life—keys, pens, glasses, cities—and then she writes "one might think this would have prepared me / for losing one average-sized not exceptionally / beautiful or dazzlingly intelligent person . . . / But it doesn't seem to have at all . . . " By the seventeenth draft, nearly every word has been transformed, but most importantly, Bishop discovered along the way that there might be a way to master this loss.

Following is the first draft of Bishop's poem. Compare this free verse version to her final, intricately crafted "One Art." Notice the compression that took place, as well as the change in thought process from the first to the final version.

Suggestions for Writing

1. Notice how Bishop's "One Art" and Cope's "Lonely Hearts" (both villanelles) are developed via a "listing" effect. Make a list (of at least twenty lines) in your journal. For instance, you might try a topic such as "things I should have said to him," or "bits of gossip." As you work with the list, see if a refrain begins to naturally emerge. As you discard or add, see how the drafts begin to change. What discoveries did you make in the process of reworking?

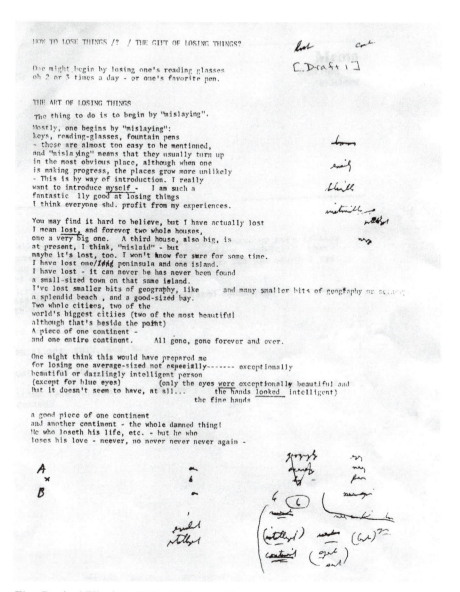

First Draft of Elizabeth Bishop's "One Art"

2. Choose one of your own poems for which the process of revision
   has been giving you difficulty. It may not have found its best form
   or incarnation. Put the poem aside and begin again. Perhaps write
   the poem from a different viewpoint (e.g., use the grandmother's
   voice instead of the father's) or make it more of a narrative instead
   of focusing on a lyrical moment.

What's in a Name:
Finding a Title

Read/Revisit

Craig Raine, "A Martian Sends a Postcard Home" (see page 202)
William Stafford, "Traveling through the Dark" (see page 210)

An important aspect of revision can be finding a title for your work. Maxine Kumin says that titles are "geography, chronology, or furniture." By furniture, she means some element present in the poem that becomes the title. In a poem like Craig Raine's "A Martian Sends a Postcard Home," the title tells us precisely where we are, and the poem itself can become the postcard home. William Stafford's title "Traveling through the Dark" has resonance on more than one level. It tells us where we are and what we are doing, but it has evocative, symbolic interpretations as well.

Alice Munro's short story "How I Met My Husband" adds another dimension to the possibilities of a title. The title of this story lures the reader into believing that the romance being described throughout the story will lead to the marriage, when, in actuality, only the final paragraph of the story introduces the main character's prospective husband. The title serves the purpose of misleading the reader so we are further drawn into the twists and turns of the main character's experiences.

A title can also serve subtle but symbolic purposes. Evan Connell selected *Mrs. Bridge* as both the name of his main character and the name of his book because of the bridge-playing, country club society he was exposing. He was also implying the social reality that one could ignore "less pleasant" aspects of society by simply crossing over them on a bridge.

Sometimes a title arrives early in the process. But more often the selection of titles can make for a good story in itself. The title of James M. Cain's famous novel *The Postman Always Rings Twice* (adapted into two movies, a play, and an opera) has an intriguing story. Cain gave two different accounts of the origin of the title. He said that while he was working on the novel, the postman would ring twice if the mail carried bills and once if a personal letter. The arrival of bills every day drove the writer into a state of frustration as he worked on his novel. But in Cain's other account of the title's genesis, he says that the postman would ring twice if he carried rejection letters and once if an acceptance letter. When Cain's novel was accepted, and the doorbell rang once, he celebrated by giving the novel its name.

Suggestions for Writing

1. Take a piece of your writing that has, in your opinion or others', a mediocre working title. Apply Kumin's concept of "geography, chronology, or furniture." Give the piece a title that places us somewhere. Now find the "furniture"; look for an extraordinary line or image already present in the writing that might work as the title. If you do use it as the title, you might consider removing it from the text.

2. Try a symbolic title. Can you identify a particular element in the piece that has resonance on both a literal level as well as a symbolic one?

Finding the Form:
A Revision Narrative

Read/Revisit

Diane Thiel, "*Memento Mori* in Middle School" (see page 213)

For years, I had the idea to write about a memory of an odd middle school project I did on Dante's *Inferno*. The narrative itself existed (in my mind and my memory), but the piece hadn't yet quite found its form. Would it be cast as an essay, a story, a poem? Choosing poetry to tell the story of first encountering Dante's epic seemed most appropriate, but the choice of terza rima for the poem occurred later in the process. An early draft of the poem is reproduced on the pages following. It is not the first draft (I write everything initially by hand) but the first typed draft.

In the early stages of writing a poem, I often find myself putting "Notes for a Poem" at the top of the page because I hardly think of the draft as a poem, but more as a free-write. As I looked through the twenty-some drafts of this poem, I chose this one to illustrate the revision process because it is the point at which a crucial realization about the form of the poem took place. What could I do with this story? How should I render it? And then it came to me—terza rima—of course! The form Dante invented for *The Divine Comedy* suddenly seemed the only choice! The form is particularly suited to narratives because its interlocking rhyme scheme provides a natural forward motion. I knew it should work well for my telling this story.

In the first typed lines of this draft, as well as in my handwritten reworking in the lower right-hand corner, you can see the new incarnation of the poem beginning to take shape. The first lines are rewritten with a tentative terza rima, testing out the new idea. Subsequent drafts show my reworking of various parts of the poem to arrive, finally, at a version of terza rima. I say "version" because, although the lines in the finished poem are metrical and rhymed, the rhymes are often somewhat muted. You can see, even in this early reworking of the opening, that I chose to soften the rhymes into *chimes*, perhaps, by using assonance and off-rhyme. The exact rhymes then attain a more emphatic quality when they are heard.

Most of the narrative details are already present in this early draft. In the case of this particular poem, the introduction (or deletion of events and ideas) was not a crucial part of the revision. Creating the poem had to do, mostly, with finding the right lyrical path. The heightening and clarification of certain details, however, became an important aspect of revision. In the second line of the poem, for instance, adding the small detail about "gifted class" gives the narrative more credibility. An average class of twelve-year-olds would not be reading the *Inferno*. The detail also begins establishing the tongue-in-cheek tone. How odd those gifted-class projects (and students) were! The union of the *Inferno* with that trial-filled middle school age became a reflection of threshold crossings that burn themselves into our memories.

One important point that had to be expanded in later drafts was the introduction of Fred, whom the children thought of at the wood of suicides. In the early draft, the narrative moves quickly past what may have happened to him, but this detail becomes the dark heart, the *memento mori* (recognition of our mortality), perhaps even the motivation for the poem. The mention of Fred needed a longer moment to reverberate.

The change in title from "Presenting the Divine Comedy" to "*Memento Mori* in Middle School" reflects the importance of this point in the narrative and sets up both the dark and the light in the poem. You can see the new title making its first appearance at the top of the second page of the draft, close to the point where Fred is introduced. The lighter aspects of the poem, with all the details about a child's interpretation of Dante's poem, might make a reader laugh aloud, but the suggestion of Fred's likely suicide gives the poem important contrasting darker shades.

Suggestions for Writing

1. Take a poem you are working on and try recasting it. Does the form you have chosen thus far serve the poem thematically? Are there any repetitions of themes, lines, or words that might suggest using a form of repetition, such as a villanelle or sestina? If it is a narrative, you might want to consider terza rima, the ballad, or blank verse. Look closely at any rhythm or rhyme scheme that may be trying to emerge in your draft.

2. Look at a short piece of your writing (from your journal or perhaps a more developed piece). What details are most crucial to creating the tone or tones of the piece? Do any important details need further elaboration?

3. An important aspect of revision is knowing when to stop, an issue that often troubles both beginning and established writers. Save drafts of each poem and number them. You may find yourself returning to earlier drafts, or at least sections of earlier drafts. It is useful to put poems aside for a while before revising. Take a particular poem that has several drafts and write a short piece of prose describing what your revision process has been with the poem. You might begin to notice your own patterns of revision.

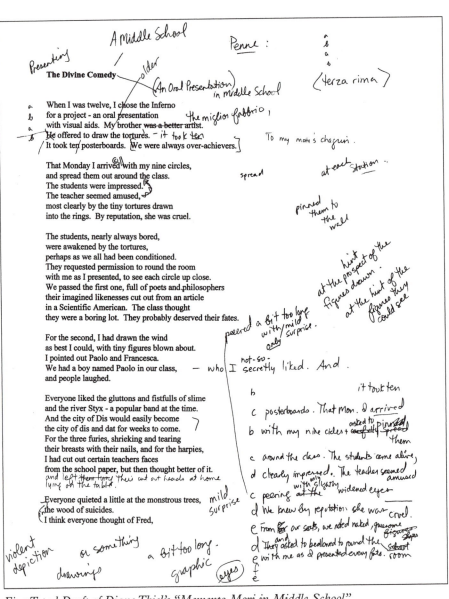

The Divine Comedy

When I was twelve, I chose the Inferno
for a project - an oral presentation
with visual aids. My brother was a better artist.
He offered to draw the tortures. - it took ten
It took ten posterboards. We were always over-achievers.

That Monday I arrived with my nine circles,
and spread them out around the class.
The students were impressed.
The teacher seemed amused,
most clearly by the tiny tortures drawn
into the rings. By reputation, she was cruel.

The students, nearly always bored,
were awakened by the tortures,
perhaps as we all had been conditioned.
They requested permission to round the room
with me as I presented, to see each circle up close.
We passed the first one, full of poets and philosophers
their imagined likenesses cut out from an article
in a Scientific American. The class thought
they were a boring lot. They probably deserved their fates.

For the second, I had drawn the wind
as best I could, with tiny figures blown about.
I pointed out Paolo and Francesca.
We had a boy named Paolo in our class,
and people laughed.

Everyone liked the gluttons and fistfulls of slime
and the river Styx - a popular band at the time.
And the city of Dis would easily become
the city of dis and dat for weeks to come.
For the three furies, shrieking and tearing
their breasts with their nails, and for the harpies,
I had cut out certain teachers faces
from the school paper, but then thought better of it.
and left them lying on the table.

Everyone quieted a little at the monstrous trees,
the wood of suicides.
I think everyone thought of Fred,

First Typed Draft of Diane Thiel's "Memento Mori in Middle School"

Memento Mori

though no one said a word.

People moved on quickly to Geryon
and rode the flying monster down.
The wicked counselors we knew by name.
They occupied the office right below us.
But again, I had resisted pasting in their faces.
A last minute decision. Their little cut-out heads
remained on the table at home.

always wanted to know
what happened to
"what about those sweet
poems I used to write."

For the ice in the last circle, where my brother
had expertly drawn the traitors with unfeeling hearts,
my mother had insisted I take with me
a freezer full of popsicles — to end on a lighter note,
she said. After all, it is a comedy isn't it?
Always a bit disturbed by my projects, she hadn't seen
the end result. But she thought, by the end,
everyone would need it.

I wanted to be liked.

Encouraged by the treat, the class moved quickly
to the last circle, and chose their colors.
The teacher, mildly confused, but knowing
they would melt, reluctantly allowed them.
And when the bell announced the change of class,
we left her room with red and purple mouths.

became kids
again.

nearly forgotten

the concerns
amidst the
nearly forgotten by everyone.
I carried the posters back
home.

we all had secrets by then.

Bird
Imagery
(Penne:
wings) ...

Present some philosophy   —

A + E — fortunate fall

Francesca.

We understood descent.

and still have
them
somewhere in the house
that.

Workshop: Thirteen Ways of Looking for Revision

Writers often have a hard time evaluating their own pieces for the purpose of revising—especially pieces they have recently been working on. Workshopping offers the opportunity to get another perspective on your work, to get feedback from your potential audience. If you do not have the opportunity to participate in a formal workshop, you could ask a peer to read your piece critically. The following questions can be used by the reader of your piece to obtain insights into how the piece might be revised so it can become more effective. You may use these questions yourself, but it is often useful to attain some "distance" from your piece, perhaps by putting it aside for a period of time, before you review it.

Questions for Revising

1. What effect does the title have on the piece? Does it add anything? Could you think of something else that would serve a functional or symbolic purpose?

2. Is the opening effective? Is there another scene or image in the piece that might serve as a stronger way to begin?

3. Does the piece work best in its current form? Can you imagine another possibility for rendering it?

4. Does the chosen perspective present the piece most effectively? How would the piece work told from someone else's perspective?

5. How does the setting work for this piece? How soon, as readers, do we know where (and when) we are? How does the writer give us this information? Could it be more subtle? Direct? If the setting is generic on purpose, does this work?

6. Does the piece hold your interest throughout? What creates the dramatic tension in the piece and is there enough of it? Does the tension drop at any points? What might be done to maintain the intensity?

7. Is the language general or specific? Is it abstract or concrete? Note any abstract words that could be replaced with fresh images. Can you suggest any images?

8. Is the voice or dialogue of the speakers or characters believable? Is there consistency? What creates inconsistencies? How might this be refined? If there is meant to be intentional inconsistency, is that working?

9. Read a passage aloud. Does the language of the piece have rhythm? How might the piece be made more rhythmical?

10. How is the piece structured? Does the series of scenes or images work effectively? Can you think of another arrangement that might work better?

11. Does every word, sentence, scene have a purpose? What can be cut?

12. Is there anything that may confuse the reader unnecessarily? How might the confusing passage be clarified?

13. Does the closure reverberate? Does it effectively give an ending without restating too much? Does it leave the reader thinking? Is this piece really finished, or could you envision a different, more effective ending? Does the piece go on beyond what might be a more effective closure?

PART TWO

Exercises in Form and Structure

14

Free Verse:
Origins and Seasons

Read/Revisit

W. H. Auden, "Musée des Beaux Arts" (see page 160)
Carolyn Forché, "The Colonel" (see page 175)
Walt Whitman, "When I Heard the Learned Astronomer" (see page 217)

Free verse is the translation of *vers libre*, which arose in France in the late nineteenth century, partially in response to strict structural rules for poetry regarding such things as precise placement of caesura (or pause) in the line, and counting of syllables. Vers libre began as a relaxation of these rules. The early twentieth century in America brought free verse to the forefront, and the new philosophy about poetry was encapsulated in Ezra Pound's famous statement that one should "compose in the sequence of the musical phrase, not the metronome."

The name *free verse*, however, has often been debated and called inaccurate and misleading because it implies that there are no limitations or guiding principles. Other terms are sometimes preferred—*open form poetry*, for instance.

Ironically, memorable poetry in open form can be very difficult to write because of the discipline that such freedom demands. The unit of free verse is often described as being a breath. The form requires an attention to the cadences of language. Each phrase should be weighed carefully, as should the length of a line. Rhythm is a vital aspect of open form. One of the dangers of free verse is that it sometimes implies to beginners that "anything goes." Much poetry being written today exists on the page, but not in the ear. Arbitrary line breaks and a lack of rhythm can be the unfortunate result.

As any teacher knows, students sometimes want to declare "open season" on all rules (grammatical, formal, etc.). However, certain "seasons" in one's writing can be useful (as many exercises in this book suggest). It is important to remember (though I don't love extending the hunting metaphor) that open season does not mean obliterating all of the animals in the forest.

When discussing the origins of free verse, it is vital to remember that the poets who introduced it into their contemporary society had been trained in traditional forms. Poets such as Whitman, Pound, Eliot, and

Stevens have undercurrents of form in their free verse. But even earlier "formal" poets such as John Milton, William Blake, and Matthew Arnold used radical departures from meter or rhyme schemes before such action had name and popularity.

There are different conjectures as to the reasons for the development of free verse in America. American writers may have been endeavoring to cast off English forms. Walt Whitman is often named as our most familiar American writer of free verse. The great musicality and rhythm in his lines are often said to reflect the landscapes of his American heritage. His lines often have a rising quality or a falling quality, based on the rhythm. One often hears pairs of lines with the same meter. Whitman often creates rhythms using parallel structures. In "When I Heard the Learned Astronomer," for instance, notice the way the rhythm builds with the increasing number of beats in the first few lines.

Whitman also employs other techniques of repetition to make rhythm, such as the grammatical use of the present participle to achieve a "continual" effect, as in the following lines from "Song of Myself":

> Many sweating, ploughing, thrashing, and then the chaff for
>   payment receiving.
> A few idly owning, and they the wheat continually claiming.
>
> WALT WHITMAN (1819–1892)

Poems in open form sometimes follow a basic metrical pattern and might occasionally be characterized in metrical terms. A poem might be said to have a loose *dactylic* rhythm, for instance (see the chapter on "Hearing the Beat: Using Meter").

Poetry often has an attention to the shape on the page, which translates to the ear. *Visual* or *concrete* poetry is the term for the particular kind of poetry in which the words form actual shapes: a bird, wings, a flower, etc. But any open form poetry can take on interesting shapes based on subject, and all should have good reason for their line breaks. May Swenson's "The Shape of Death" is an example of a poem whose form on the page was altered to create a distinct rhythm and meaning. Swenson wrote the poem ten years after the bombing of Hiroshima and Nagasaki. Originally, the poem was structured:

> there is a clap of sound, a white blossom
> belches from the jaw of fright,
> a pillared cloud churns from white to gray
> like a monstrous brain that bursts and burns,
> then turns sickly black, spilling away,
> filling the whole sky with ashes of dread

In a later version, Swenson rearranged the lines of her poem, "remembering" them by dismembering them, creating the effect of what is blown apart:

There is a

clap of sound. A white	blossom belches from the
jaw of fright. A	monstrous brain that bursts
and burns—then turns	sickly black, spilling
away, filling the whole	sky with ashes of dread.

MAY SWENSON (1919–1989)

Good open form poetry has rhythm, whether it be a fluidity or an intentionally jarring pattern of sound to create a certain effect. One element is essential in all writing: poets need to train and use their ears.

Suggestions for Writing

1. Read aloud some free verse poems whose lines have remained with you. Identify any metrical patterns within (see "Hearing the Beat: Using Meter"). What kind of patterns exist? Can you identify a reason for each line break?

2. Experiment with line breaks. Consider Swenson's deliberate jarring effect in the above excerpt. Choose a subject that would benefit from such a chaotic structure and rhythm and use the line breaks to create meaning.

3. In all writing (but in free verse, in particular) the rhythm often relies on word choice or particular combinations of sound, such as internal rhyme or alliteration (see the "Committing a Rhyme"). Combinations of words can create a fluid pace or a harsh, breaking rhythm. Sometimes such rhythms appear beneath your pen. Harvest your free-writing to find some of these combinations. Build on the structures you find.

4. Notice how Auden's "Musée des Beaux Arts," though decidedly free verse, has interesting rhyme schemes throughout the poem. Notice the structure of long and short lines as well. Try Auden's use of alternating long and short lines.

15
Making and Breaking the Line

Read/Revisit

Sherman Alexie, "Indian Education" (see page 151)
William Carlos Williams, "The Dance" (see page 222)

In the previous chapter, "Free Verse," different possibilities for creating the rhythm and lyricism of a free verse poem are discussed. Attention to "the line" as poetry's main unit is of major importance to both formal and free verse poems. In much formal poetry, the line is determined by an established length and a particular rhythm that forms the foundation of its lyricism.

With free verse, attention to the line is particularly vital because much of the music is determined by the poet's choices regarding the line. When writing poetry, essentially, we "teach" the reader how to read the poem by where we break the line, often using an unexpected pause to achieve a certain effect.

In Sherman Alexie's "Indian Education," for instance, note how the pause created by the line break allows for a moment of expectation to build from the first line of Alexie's poem:

Crazy Horse came back to life
in a storage room of the Smithsonian

The poem also closes with particularly evocative line breaks:

although Crazy Horse measured himself
against the fact of a mirror, traded faces
with a taxi driver and memorized the city,
folding, unfolding, his mapped heart.

The line breaks allow each idea of how Crazy Horse "measured himself" and then "traded faces" to reverberate for a moment before the poem moves on to the mirror and the taxi driver. The measured pauses allow the final stanza to build toward the striking closing image of "his mapped heart."

In "A Supermarket in California," Allen Ginsberg, in writing about Walt Whitman, emulates Whitman's long lines, lists, and parallel structures. Ginsberg's choice of line length has the effect of establishing an affinity with Whitman on a level deeper than the imagined appearance of Whitman in the supermaket.

William Carlos Williams's poem "The Dance" (discussed also in "Rhythm and Refrain") has intriguing line breaks that suit its subject matter. Note how lines two and three seem to break in odd places:

> In Brueghel's great picture, The Kermess,
> the dancers go round, they go round and
> around, the squeal and the blare and the
> tweedle of bagpipes

What could be the reason for these odd line breaks? What might they have to do with the subject matter of the poem?

Suggestions for Writing

1. Study the Williams poem mentioned above. Now write a few lines that depict a particular movement (e.g., a dance, running long distance, climbing a ladder). Play with the line breaks to depict the movement that is the subject of the poem.

2. Look at the poems noted above. Do you see other particular reasons the poet breaks the line where he or she does? Take a poem you have written and experiment with breaking the lines differently. Have someone else read it aloud in its original form and with its different line breaks. How does it change the reading of the poem?

16
Parallel Structures

Read/Revisit

Joy Harjo, "She Had Some Horses" (see page 183)
Sherman Alexie, "Indian Education" (see page 151)
Sherman Alexie and Diane Thiel, "A Conversation with Sherman Alexie" (see page 152)
Wallace Stevens, "Disillusionment of Ten O'Clock" (see page 211)

Parallel structures are another type of rhythmical tool in prose or poetry. The repetitions are often used to reinforce a statement and effect a certain rhythm. Great orators were known for employing this technique, such as Martin Luther King Jr. in his famous "I Have a Dream" speech and "Letter from Birmingham Jail." One well-known example of parallelism is the following verse:

For want of a nail, the shoe was lost,
For want of a shoe, the horse was lost,
For want of a horse, the rider was lost,
For want of a rider, the battle was lost,
For want of a battle, the kingdom was lost,
And all for the want of a horseshoe nail.

BENJAMIN FRANKLIN (1706–1790)

Walt Whitman often uses a parallel structure to create rhythm in his free verse. The following is an excerpt from "When Lilacs Last in the Dooryard Bloom'd," Whitman's famous elegy mourning the death of Abraham Lincoln. The repetition of the first word of a line as the first word in succeeding lines is known as *anaphora*. Notice the way the parallel structure builds the rhythm and contributes to the intensity of the traveling coffin:

Coffin that passes through lanes and streets,
Through day and night with the great cloud darkening the land,
With the pomp of the inloop'd flags with the cities draped in black,
With the show of the States themselves as of crape-veil'd women
    standing,
With processions long and winding and the flambeaus of the night,
With the countless torches lit, with the silent sea of faces and the
    unbared heads,

With the waiting depot, the arriving coffin, and the sombre faces,
With dirges through the night, with the thousand voices rising
    strong and solemn,
With all the mournful voices of the dirges pour'd around the coffin,
The dim-lit churches and the shuddering organs—where amid
    these you journey,
With the tolling bells' perpetual clang,
Here, coffin that slowly passes,
I give you my sprig of lilac.

                    WALT WHITMAN (1819–1892)

Parallel structures exist in Native American traditions as well. Joy Harjo often uses such repetition, as in "She Had Some Horses," a poem filled with contradictions:

She had horses who called themselves "horse."
She had horses who called themselves "spirit," and kept
their voices secret and to themselves. . . .
She had horses who whispered in the dark, who were afraid
    to speak.
She had horses who screamed out of fear of the silence, who
carried knives to protect themselves from ghosts.
She had horses who waited for destruction.
She had horses who waited for resurrection.

                    JOY HARJO (B. 1951)

Sherman Alexie uses similar parallel structures in many of his poems, as in "Indian Education," where the repetition of "Crazy Horse" creates an element of rhythm in the poem. In the interview included in the collection of readings in Part Three, Alexie speaks about his artistic and cultural reasons for using parallel structure and repetition.

Many writers also use a parallel structure called *chiasmus* (crossing), in which the word order of one phrase is inverted in the next, as in the lines that open Christian Wiman's long narrative poem in blank verse, "The Long Home." The effect is one of elegance within simple language:

We drove all day on roads without a speck
Of paving, not knowing but knowing not
to ask when we would stop or where.

                    CHRISTIAN WIMAN (B. 1966)

A good example of chiasmus in prose is the following sentence from Marilynne Robinson's novel *Housekeeping*: "Every sorrow suggests a thousand songs, and every song recalls a thousand sorrows."

Suggestions for Writing

1. Write a short free-write using a parallel structure to emphasize your point and give the passage a certain rhythm.

2. To practice chiasmus, list several pairs of words that create an interesting meaning or rhythm. The word "not" works well with many different verbs, but also try to think of some other pairings. Now incorporate each set into a line. A caution: chiasmus can add spice to writing, but just a pinch is often enough.

3. When we describe something, our natural tendency is to list its characteristics. But it can be powerful to describe something by stating what it is not. Use Wallace Stevens's "Disillusionment of Ten O'Clock" as a model and create a parallel structure of negative statements.

17

Stanzas

Many poems (open form poems as well as those with more traditional forms) are organized in stanzas, or groups of lines. *Stanza* comes from the Italian, meaning "room, or stopping place." The following is a very brief overview of stanza forms with a few examples, as well as a few suggestions of other poems to seek out on your own. The overview is intended to give you a sense of the way you might break your own poems into traditional stanza forms, or use such structures as points of departure. Poems broken into stanzas need not necessarily rhyme, of course, but the following examples offer both classical and contemporary examples of rhyme.

Some poems are arranged in *couplets* (units of two lines), from the heroic verse of Dryden and Pope to such familiar poems as Blake's "The Tyger." Often couplets are distinguished only by the rhyme scheme (aabbcc, etc.) rather than visual space. Some couplets, however, are arranged in a structure of two-line stanzas, as in Rhina P. Espaillat's "Bilingual/Bilingüe."

My father liked them separate, one there,
one here (allá y aquí), as if aware

that words might cut in two his daughter's heart
(el corazón) and lock the alien part

RHINA P. ESPAILLAT (B. 1932)

Three-line stanzas, or *tercets*, might carry different rhyme schemes, or all three lines of the tercet might rhyme:

The Angel that presided o'er my birth
Said little creature formed of joy and mirth
Go love without the help of anything on earth.

WILLIAM BLAKE (1757–1827)

The following example breaks the rhythm and alters the rhyme for the purpose of slowing the poem down at its closure:

Stillness after motion,
the creaky music cranking, cranking down,
the carnival preparing to leave town.

RACHEL HADAS (B. 1948)

99

Another common rhyme scheme for a three-line stanza is terza rima (triple rhyme) such as Dante used. The rhyme scheme is aba, bcb, cdc, etc., and the middle rhyme of each tercet becomes the first and third rhyme of the next stanza. The interlocking form weaves the stanzas together and gives the poem movement, propelling it forward.

Marilyn Nelson's "Chosen" uses tercets with a varying rhyme scheme to form part of a sonnet. For a variation on terza rima, see my poem, "Memento Mori in Middle School." (Both are included in Part Three.)

The quatrain, or four-line stanza, is the most common in European literature. A common quatrain is the ballad stanza, with four beats in the first and third lines, and three (sometimes four) beats in the second and fourth lines. Emily Dickinson used this form in most of her poems. Note the structure and rhythm of the following stanzas from Nikos Kavadias's "A Knife":

> I remember, as if it were now, the old dealer
> who looked like a Goya oil painting,
> standing next to long swords and torn
> uniforms—in a hoarse voice, saying,
>
> "This knife, here, which you want to buy—
> legend surrounds it. Everyone knows
> that those who have owned it, one after another
> have all, at some time, killed someone close.

NIKOS KAVADIAS (1913–1975)
TRANSLATED BY DIANE THIEL

The five-line stanza allows for many combinations of rhymes and line lengths. Edgar Allan Poe uses the familiar quatrain and adds an additional rhyming line:

To Helen

> Helen, thy beauty is to me
>   Like those Nicéan barks of yore,
> That gently, o'er a perfumed sea,
>   The weary, way-worn wanderer bore
>   To his own native shore.
>
> On desperate seas long wont to roam,
>   Thy hyacinth hair, thy classic face,
> Thy Naiad airs have brought me home
>   To the glory that was Greece,
>   And the grandeur that was Rome.
>
> Lo! in yon brilliant window-niche
>   How statue-like I see thee stand,

The agate lamp within thy hand!
Ah, Psyche, from the regions which
    Are Holy-Land!

EDGAR ALLAN POE (1809–1849)

For another example of the five-line stanza, see Robert Frost's "The Road Not Taken" (included in Part Three).

The six-line stanza might contain one of many different patterns of rhyme and meter. The "Venus and Adonis" stanza, named for Shakespeare's poem, is a quatrain with a couplet: ababcc. The "Burns stanza" or "Scottish stanza" follows a pattern of aaabab—the a lines are tetrameter (four feet), the b lines are dimeter (two feet). R. S. Gwynn's "The Classroom at the Mall" uses a rhyme scheme of abccab:

Our Dean of Something thought it would be good
For Learning (even better for P.R.)
To make the school "accessible to all"
And leased the bankrupt bookstore at the Mall
A few steps from Poquito's Mexican Food
And Chocolate Chips Aweigh. So here we are—

R. S. GWYNN (B. 1948)

The *sestina* is a type of poem that uses six-line stanzas in which end words repeat in a precise pattern. There is a section on the sestina in the "Forms from Various Cultures and Traditions" chapter.

The seven-line stanza also offers many possibilities. *Rime royal* (so named because it was used by British King James I) is the most common. It contains iambic pentameter, rhyming ababbcc. But many contemporary poets have created their own seven-line structures:

My frowning students carve
Me monsters out of prose:
This one—a gargoyle—thumbs its contemptuous nose
At how, in English, subject must agree
With verb—for any such agreement shows
    Too great a willingness to serve,
        A docility

CHARLES MARTIN (B. 1942)

Ottava rima is the most widely known eight-line stanza: iambic pentameter, abababcc—familiar to many through Yeats's "Among School Children" and Byron's witty *Don Juan*:

His classic studies made a little puzzle,
    Because of filthy loves of gods and goddesses,

Who in the earlier ages raised a bustle,
> But never put on pantaloons or bodices;
His reverend tutors had at times a tussle,
> And for their Aeneiads, Iliads and Odysseys,
Were forced to make an odd sort of apology,
> For Donna Inez dreaded the Mythology.

GEORGE GORDON, LORD BYRON (1788–1824)

Fred D'Aguiar's *Bloodlines* is a contemporary narrative in ottava rima:

And now I have to make a confession.
I said way back that I can't die, sure,
but the real truth is I won't die, not as long
as slavery harnesses history, driving her
over the edge, into the ground, to exhaustion.
I refuse to lie in ground whose pressure,
shaped like my body, is not six feet of soil,
but slavery; not history on me, but forced toil.

FRED D'AGUIAR (B. 1960)

Timothy Steele's "The Library" is a good contemporary example of a nine-line stanza:

I could construct a weighty paradigm,
The Library as Mind. It's somehow truer
To recollect details of closing time.
Someone, at slotted folders on a viewer,
Tucks microfiche squares in their resting places;
Felt cloth's drawn over the exhibit cases;
The jumbled New Book Shelves are set in shape;
The days' last check-outs are thumped quickly through a
Device that neutralizes tattle-tape.

TIMOTHY STEELE (B. 1948)

The Spenserian stanza (used in Edmund Spenser's *The Faerie Queen*) is a special nine-line form. The first eight lines are iambic pentameter and the ninth is an alexandrine (with twelve syllables). The rhyme scheme is ababbcbcc. Byron, Shelley, and other Romantics enjoyed the elaborate musical quality of the interlacing form. The following is the first stanza of Shelley's famous elegy for John Keats, "Adonais":

I weep for Adonais—he is dead!
Oh, weep for Adonais! though our tears
Thaw not the frost which binds so dear a head!
And thou sad Hour, selected from all years

To mourn our loss, rouse thy obscure compeers,
And teach them thine own sorrow, say: with me
Died Adonais; till the Future dares
Forget the Past, his fate and fame shall be
An echo and a light unto eternity!

PERCY BYSSHE SHELLEY (1792–1822)

For more about elegies, see the "Occasionals" section in the chapter on "Forms from Various Cultures and Traditions."

Some forms of poetry have no fixed stanzas; they continue until they end. *Blank verse* (unrhymed iambic pentameter) is the best known pattern for poems in English. Most parts of Shakespeare's plays are in blank verse, as is Milton's *Paradise Lost.* Many twentieth-century writers, such as Robert Frost and Elizabeth Bishop, found blank verse an ideal form for conveying the natural rhythms of language. (See, for instance, Frost's "Out Out," included in Part Three. Frost found the subject for this chilling poem in a newspaper article and rendered the subject matter in blank verse.)

Numerous contemporary writers, such as Mark Jarman, Emily Grosholz, Dave Mason, Mary Jo Salter, and Christian Wiman (to name just a few), continue in this tradition, often using the blank verse form to sustain longer narrative poems, sometimes book-length works.

Suggestions for Writing

Try your hand at the different stanza forms. Pay attention to certain shapes and structures that may emerge in your journal. Notice, for instance, if a poem seems to be developing in couplets. Model your favorite poets. You will probably find that certain divisions suit your particular voice or certain subjects better than others.

18
Rhythm and Refrain

Read/Revisit
    Yusef Komunyakaa, "Rhythm Method" (see page 191)
    Michael S. Harper, "Dear John, Dear Coltrane" (see page 185)
    Alfonsina Storni, "Ancestral Burden" (see page 212)
    William Carlos Williams, "The Dance" (see page 222)
    Naomi Shihab Nye, "Famous" (see page 201)

As discussed briefly in the sections on "Free Verse," "Making and Breaking the Line," and "Parallel Structures" in particular, there are a variety of inventive ways to create rhythm in a free verse poem. Yusef Komunyakaa, in "Rhythm Method," speaks of the organic nature of rhythm, how we feel it in every aspect of our lives:

If you can see the blues
in the ocean, light & dark,
can feel worms ease through
a subterranean path
beneath each footstep,
Baby, you got rhythm.

Sometimes the rhythm of a free verse poem has an undercurrent of a formal element, such as the undercurrent of the triple rhythms in William Carlos Williams's "The Dance." In Alfonsina Storni's "Ancestral Burden," note how both the repetition in the first few lines, as well as the structure of the sapphic-like stanza (after Sappho, with three longer lines and then a short one), creates a unique rhythmical effect:

You told me my father never cried
You told me my grandfather never cried
The men of my lineage never cried
They were steel inside.

A number of writers have "found their rhythm" in various poems via inspiration from sources such as jazz refrains. Michael S. Harper's "Dear John, Dear Coltrane" names its influence quite directly in the title. Consider how the poem itself feels like a jazz tune. Note the repetitions throughout the poem. When Harper reads this poem, he performs it, singing the refrain:

a love supreme
a love supreme
a love supreme

Suggestions for Writing

1. Listen to jazz for inspiration. Try to emulate some of the rhythms you hear as you free-write in your journal. Follow a pattern and then break off in an unexpected direction.

2. Yusef Komunyakaa refers to a series of natural rhythms in the world, creating a list. What rhythms in the natural world have you been conscious of? The rain? The ocean? Make a short list. Now try writing a few lines that emulate one of these sources of rhythm.

3. Naomi Shihab Nye's repetition of "famous" creates a poignant and rhythmical effect in "Famous." Try emulating her use of repetition in the poem.

4. In Williams's "The Dance," consider the undercurrent of rhythm throughout the poem. How do the triple rhythms affect the subject matter: a dance? Write some lines of free verse in which the rhythm carries an emphatic meaning.

19
Hearing the Beat: Using Meter

Rhythmical patterns of poetry are referred to as *meter* (from the Greek, meaning "measure"). Hearing or reciting a poem with meter gives us a physical as well as an intellectual or emotional pleasure. Theorists have different conjectures about this physical reaction. Some suggest that it has to do with meter's hypnotic power. Others suggest that because the accents in much metered verse are faster than our heartbeats, they excite and speed up our hearts.

Frederick Turner, in his essay "The Neural Lyre," speaks about the effect of metered verse on the brain—that it encourages the left brain to communicate with the right brain. He suggests that our left-brain activity of understanding language becomes infused with our more hard-wired, right-brain pattern-recognition abilities, that meter, essentially, tunes up the brain, combining a rhythmic organization with a variety of syntactical possibilities. He speaks of the brain as a "*Penelope*, whose right hand weaves the shroud of meaning and whose left hand disentangles the thread or clue of understanding."

Turner traces how societies have evolved using meter, a cultural universal, perhaps because of its hypnotic power to cast a spell in the mind—a rhythmic reality rooted in science. Dana Gioia, in *Can Poetry Matter*, draws on this recognition of meter as an ancient technique used when there was very "little, if any distinction among poetry, religion, history, music, and magic." All were performed using an incantatory meter.

Poetry written with meter is sometimes called *verse*, from the Latin *versus*, meaning "turned around or back." The structural unit of the line in most poetry (metered or unmetered) has this element of the "turn." The word *line* derives from the Latin *linea*, associated with linen, or thread. One might think of poetry as lines spun together on a loom. The rhythms of language have meaning and are a powerful element of the weave.

It is a good idea to become familiar with the various meters (both the patterns of regularity as well as different methods of variation) and to try your hand at them. It will help you recognize why certain lines have always remained with you, and it will give you additional tools for writing. You may even begin to notice meter in prose passages or in everyday speech. Many lines of everyday speech in English, for instance, tend to be iambic, a pattern of alternating unstressed and stressed syllables.

The Basic Patterns

The unit whose repetition creates the rhythm in a line is called a *foot*. Following are examples of iambic, trochaic, anapestic, and dactylic feet. Boldface type in the examples indicates a stressed syllable, and words have been broken up to show the individual syllables in some of the lines.

Iambic lines consist primarily of *iambs*. An iamb is an unstressed syllable followed by a stressed syllable.

> I **all** / a **lone** / be **weep** / my **out** / cast **state**
>
> WILLIAM SHAKESPEARE (1564–1616)

> Woke **up** / this **mor** / nin', **blues** / all **round** / my **bed**
>
> TRADITIONAL BLUES LYRIC

Trochaic lines consist mainly of *trochees*. A trochee is a stressed syllable followed by an unstressed syllable. Trochaic meter is often used to convey a kind of mystical quality, as in the following:

> **Once** up / **on** a / **mid** night / **drear** y, / **while** I / **pon** dered, /
>   **weak** and / **wear** y,
> Over many a quaint and curious volume of forgotten lore—
> While I nodded, nearly napping, suddenly there came a tapping,
> As of someone gently rapping, rapping at my chamber door.
> "Tis some visitor," I muttered, "tapping at my chamber door—
> Only this and nothing more."
>
> EDGAR ALLAN POE (1809–1849)

Anapestic lines consist mainly of *anapests*. An anapest is two unstressed syllables followed by a stressed syllable. Note the galloping pace of these lines from Robert Browning's "How We Brought the Good News from Ghent to Aix," created by the use of the anapest:

> And his **low** / head and **crest**, / just one **sharp** / ear bent **back**
> For my voice, and the other pricked out on his track;
> And one eye's black intelligence,—ever that glance
> O'er its white edge at me, his own master, askance!
>
> ROBERT BROWNING (1812–1889)

In "Confederacy," by contemporary poet Elise Paschen, the anapests feel like a dance, like Paschen's "two-stepping" subject:

> Wear the **heart** / like a **home**
> as in Patsy Kline's song,
> what we're two-stepping to
>
> ELISE PASCHEN (B. 1959)

Dactylic lines consist mainly of *dactyls*. A dactyl is one stressed syllable followed by two unstressed syllables.

> **This** is the / **for** est pri / **me** val. The / **mur** mur ing / **pines** and
> the / **hem** lock
>
> HENRY WADSWORTH LONGFELLOW (1807–1882)

June Jordan chose to use dactyls in her poem for Phyllis Wheatley—the poet slave who, in the eighteenth century, was the first woman, as well as the first African American, to publish a book in North America. Jordan's choice of form for this poem echoes Wheatley's poetry:

> **Viewed** like a / **spe** cies of / **flaw** in the / **live** stock
>
> JUNE JORDAN (B. 1936)

Variations in Meter

Variations in regularity—or metrical substitutions—are a vital aspect of meter. There are many ways one can create variation. In iambic meter, for instance, trochaic feet often appear at the beginning of lines for emphasis. In "Bilingual/Bilingüe," the trochaic feet, "English" and "Spanish" further emphasize the imperative in her father's words.

> To what he was—his memory, his name
> (su nombre)—with a key he could not claim
>
> "**Eng**lish / out**side** / this **door**, / **Span**ish / in**side**,"
>
> RHINA P. ESPAILLAT (B. 1932)

The *pyrrhic* unit is another common substitution, consisting of two unstressed syllables, as in "dom for" below":

> A **horse**! / A **Horse**! / My **king** / dom for / a **horse**!
>
> WILLIAM SHAKESPEARE (1564–1616)

The *spondee* contains two stressed syllables, as in "full kiss" below:

> Yet **once** / more **ere** / thou **hate** / me, **one** / **full kiss**.
>
> ALGERNON CHARLES SWINBURNE (1837–1909)

In "Single Sonnet," Bogan struggles with what she calls the "heroic mould" of the sonnet, which "proves" its strength and returns to iambic in her final line:

> **Staunch me**ter, **great song**, it is **yours**, at **length**,
> To **prove** how **strong**er **you** are **than** my **strength**.
>
> LOUISE BOGAN (1897–1970)

Two other ways to add variety to a line are use of the *caesura*, or pause, usually indicated by punctuation, and use of *enjambment*, or running on to the next line without a pause (as opposed to using an *end-stopped* line). The following two lines illustrate both devices:

> Lose something every day. Accept the fluster
> of lost door keys, the hour badly spent.
>
> ELIZABETH BISHOP (1911–1979)

Samuel Taylor Coleridge wrote the following lines to help memorize the different feet. Each line depicts the type of foot it describes:

> Trochee trips from long to short;
> From long to long in solemn sort
> Slow Spondee stalks, strong foot, yet ill able
> Ever to come up with Dactyl trisyllable.
> Iambics march from short to long;
> With a leap and a bound the swift Anapests throng.
>
> SAMUEL TAYLOR COLERIDGE (1772–1834)

Iambic and anapestic feet are called *rising* feet, as they move from unstressed to stressed syllables. Trochaic and dactylic feet are called *falling*. Timothy Steele comments that he sees the meter of lines as landscape, with hills and valleys of different size or levels of stress. The feet create the basic pattern, which then allows certain variations to have more impact. The amount of variation in a poem can range from very little to extensive changes, often depending on the subject.

The Basic Metrical Lines

The length of a line is essential to the rhythm of metered poetry as well as open form. (In open form, in particular, a line might break at a certain, perhaps unexpected point for the purpose of creating a particular rhythm or meaning—see the "Free Verse" chapter.) Pentameter, the most common meter, contains five feet. Monometer, dimeter, trimeter, tetrameter, hexameter, heptameter, and octameter contain one, two, three, four, six, seven, and eight beats, respectively.

Monometer (one beat), a rare line length, is used in the following epigram:

> Adam
> Had 'em.
>
> ANONYMOUS

For more about epigrams, see the chapter "Forms from Various Cultures and Traditions."

Dimeter (two beats) is used in the following lines from Tennyson's "The Charge of the Light Brigade." Note that the basic pattern is dactylic.

Cannon to right of them,
Cannon to left of them,
Cannon in front of them
Volleyed and thundered;

ALFRED, LORD TENNYSON (1809–1892)

Trimeter (three beats) is used in the lines below. Read the lines aloud and note where the stresses fall, as in the words "Up," "bronze," and "saw" in the first line.

Up from the bronze, I saw
Water without a flaw

LOUISE BOGAN (1897–1970)

Tetrameter (four beats) is used in the following quatrain. Note how the lines have four feet and an iambic pattern, which creates four stresses in each line.

Whose woods these are, I think I know.
His house is in the village, though;
He will not see me stopping here
To watch his woods fill up with snow.

ROBERT FROST (1874–1963)

Pentameter (five beats) is the most common line in English. This brief example is from Milton's *Paradise Lost* (Book IX, lines 115–123). Notice, however, that the fourth and ninth lines of the excerpt break the meter and have six beats. (The list of "rocks, dens, and caves" recalls an earlier description in Book II of the epic: "Rocks, caves, lakes, fens, bogs, dens, and shades of death"—see octameter, below.)

If I could joy in aught; sweet interchange
Of hill and valley, rivers, woods, and plains,
Now land, now sea, and shores with forest crowned,
Rocks, dens, and caves! But I in none of these
Find place or refuge; and, the more I see
Pleasures about me, so much more I feel
Torment within me, as from the hateful siege
Of contraries; all good to me becomes
Bane, and in Heaven much worse would be my state.

JOHN MILTON (1608–1674)

Hexameter (six beats), sometimes called an *alexandrine*, is used in the following stanza from "The Lake Isle of Innisfree":

> I will arise and go now, and go to Innisfree,
> And a small cabin build there, of clay and wattles made.
> Nine bean-rows will I have there, a hive for the honey-bee,
> And live alone in the bee-loud glade.
>
> WILLIAM BUTLER YEATS (1865–1939)

Heptameter (seven beats) lines, often called *fourteeners*, were common in the Renaissance but are rather uncommon now. "Casey at the Bat" is a famous American poem in heptameter:

> The outlook wasn't brilliant for the Mudville nine that day;
> The score stood four to two with but one inning more to play.
>
> ERNEST LAWRENCE THAYER (1863–1940)

Some metrists suggest that ballad meter is a derivation of heptameter, with its pattern of four stresses, then three, as in the following excerpt from "The Rime of the Ancient Mariner":

> Since then, at an uncertain hour,
> That agony returns:
> And till my ghastly tale is told,
> This heart within me burns.
>
> SAMUEL TAYLOR COLERIDGE (1772–1834)

Octameter (eight beats) is a very uncommon line in English. Swinburne's "March" is one example. Some octameter lines exist as a dramatic variation from the basic pattern of a poem, such as this line from Book II of *Paradise Lost*, which varies from the poem's basic meter (see pentameter, above):

> Rocks, caves, lakes, fens, bogs, dens, and shades of death.
>
> JOHN MILTON (1608–1674)

Lines longer than eight beats exist, but they are quite rare, probably because of the limitations imposed by the natural rhythm of breathing.

Other Metrical Lines

Some poets, such as W. H. Auden, Marianne Moore, and Dylan Thomas, have enjoyed working in **syllabic verse**, arranging lines by the number of syllables but without attention to meter. A well-known syllabic poem is Dylan Thomas's "Fern Hill." Note in these first two lines how each contains fourteen syllables:

> Now as I was young and easy under the apple boughs
> About the lilting house and happy as the grass was green
>
> Dylan Thomas (1914–1953)

Syllabic verse is sometimes confused with accentual verse. **Accentual verse** refers to the amount and pattern of stresses, not merely the number of syllables. Ballad meter, for instance, contains a wide variety of syllable counts per line, but there is a precise pattern of stresses or accents. (See the "Ballad and Ballade" section in "Forms from Various Cultures and Traditions.") Richard Wilbur's "Junk" is a good example of a contemporary use of accentual meter, with four beats in each two-part line:

> An **axe an**gles
>   from my **neigh**bor's **ash**can;
>
> Richard Wilbur (b. 1921)

Accentual iambic meter is sometimes called *loose iambics*. **Accentual syllabic verse** is the term for meter that keeps a precise pattern of syllables and accents, with variation occurring in the accents. Accentual syllabic meter is the basis for standard English meters such as iambic pentameter. **Quantitative meter,** common among the classical forms of the ancient Greeks and Romans, is based on the principle of vowel length (the time it takes to say a syllable).

Sapphic verse (named for the Greek poet Sappho, but also used by Catullus and Horace) are four-line stanzas in the meter of the example below. The term *sapphics* is also used to refer to the meter of the first three lines. The English Sapphic stanza consists of three eleven-syllable lines—hendecasyllables—followed by a five-syllable line, with the stresses as noted in the first stanza of contemporary poet Annie Finch's "Sapphics for Patience":

> **Look** there—**some** thing **rests** on your **hand** and **even**
> **lingers, though** the **wind** all a**round** is **asking**
> **it** to **leave** you. **Pass**ing the **o**pen **pass**age,
> **you** have been **cho**sen.
>
> Seed. Like dust or thistle it sits so lightly
> that your hand while holding the trust of silk gets
> gentle. Seed like hope has come, making stillness.
> Wish in the quiet.
>
> If I stood there—stopped by an open passage—
> staring at my hand—which is always open—
> hopeful, maybe, not to compel you, I'd wish
> only for patience.
>
> Annie Finch (b. 1956)

A difficulty of the Sapphic stanza may be its inflexible meter (due to an attempt to imitate classical syllable quantities), which may not allow for shifts in rhythm to create meaning. Some poets have used the basic structure of the Sapphic stanza with small metrical variations, or with a looser pattern of five beats per line, for instance.

For a far more extensive discussion of the many intricacies of meter, a comprehensive source is Timothy Steele's book on meter, *All the Fun's in How You Say a Thing.*

Practicing Meter

When using meter, our minds and bodies respond to both the regularity and the change. As Robert Bridges said, the rhythm beneath allows the poem to lift off. Practicing different meters is also likely to give your free verse and your prose a more lyrical quality, as you train your ear.

Suggestions for Writing

1. Try writing lines with the different basic meters (iambic, trochaic, etc.). You might listen to everyday speech and write down lines that have a particular rhythm. One small caution (from experience): you need not mention your identification of meter to your sources. Not everyone appreciates such a discerning ear. And there's bound to be trouble if you respond to a statement like "Let's go! We're going to be late again" with "Hey, that line is iambic pentameter!"

2. Find a passage of prose in which a few sentences follow basic metrical patterns. Break them into lines and then *feet* (the metrical subdivisions of a line) and note their *scansion* (their patterns of stress).

3. Note how such elements as caesura and enjambment affect rhythm. Try writing lines with these elements. (See also the "Making Rhyme Fresh" chapter.)

4. Write a poem in iambic pentameter. Find one or more places in the poem where a break in the meter might be used to create a particular meaning (as in the examples of variation noted). Practice techniques of variation (e.g., using trochaic, pyrrhic, or spondaic feet to vary the iambic pattern).

5. Practice writing lines that have *accentual* rhythm. Create a pattern of a certain number of beats per line (e.g., tetrameter, pentameter, etc.).

6. Read your own writing aloud (poetry and prose). It will help you hear the undercurrents of your own rhythm or identify where it needs work.

20
Trochaic Meter and Spells

When we think of the incantation that accompanies a spell, we think of a hypnotic arrangement containing rhyme and meter. Scan the following lines from Poe's "The Raven." Read them aloud to hear the rhythm.

> Once upon a midnight dreary, while I pondered, weak and weary,
> Over many a quaint and curious volume of forgotten lore
>
> EDGAR ALLAN POE (1809–1849)

In Shakespeare's *Macbeth*, when the witches cast their well-known spell, the blank verse of the play changes to a trochaic meter (a pattern of alternating stressed and unstressed syllables) with rhyme and a repetition of sounds to heighten the effect of the magic. The word *trochee* derives from the Greek *trochos*, meaning "wheel." Trochees have a forward-skipping rhythm that is particularly suitable for creating a hypnotic effect.

> Eye of newt, and toe of frog,
> Wool of bat, and tongue of dog,
> Adder's fork, and blindworm's sting,
> Lizard's leg, and howlet's wing—
> For a charm of pow'rful trouble.
> Like a hell-broth boil and bubble.
> Double, double, toil and trouble,
> Fire burn and cauldron bubble.

Suggestions for Writing

Using a basic trochaic meter, write an emulation of the above spell. In the first four lines of your spell, list the necessary ingredients. Try using ingredients of this day and age. The choice of ingredients can be a good way to talk about symbol. The items used in the spell could be chosen for their symbolic purpose: a love letter, a test, a dress, eye of newt? (Hopefully not!) List the elements and procedures for the spell as a kind of recipe. Laura Esquivel's novel *Like Water for Chocolate* has this "magically real" element of symbolic food bringing about certain events.

In the second half of your spell, include an incantation (with words such as "double, double, toil and trouble") and the intent of the spell.

When I use this exercise in classes, I like to suggest that students frame their wishes in the positive (for obvious reasons). For instance, if you want to get someone out of your life, try a spell for something positive that will take the person far far away from you.

21
Committing a Rhyme

Early on in workshops, my students often ask me if they are "allowed to rhyme" in a poem. Much of the modern work they come across has no meter or rhyme, which may seem like outdated concepts. Earlier in this century, I imagine students asked for permission *not* to rhyme. Most of the models of rhyme that an average anthology contains are poems from other centuries, so when students try to use certain patterns of sound, they often write using archaic language and syntax. Many people have not come in contact with good contemporary models of poems using rhyme (other than songs, which are often considered another category). We learn by example, and it is important to learn from the great poets of our history, but also to have contemporary models.

In Bruce Meyer's interview with British poet James Fenton in the late 1980s, Fenton suggests that there are many poets writing today who are terrified of "committing a rhyme." He states that one must defy the unspoken and spoken rules of the critics and the fads:

> Absolutely defy it. If you don't defy it, you're going to be a prisoner of your time. . . . When I was teaching in Minnesota, I learned a lot about how people can be cowed into submission by critical opinion. The terror with which they treated the question of form, as if there is a question of form. There isn't a question of form. There is poetry. There is this terrific art which has been handed down from generation to generation to read with immense pleasure. But there are some people who are sitting there terrified of committing a rhyme.

Rhyme requires practice and a good ear, or it can fail miserably. A bad poem in rhyme is more loud (cacophonous, perhaps) and noticeable than a bad free verse poem, which might just quietly die on the page. English is a difficult language in which to use rhyme, for it contains far fewer rhyming words when compared with Spanish or Italian, for instance. Variations broaden the musical possibilities in English and often allow for lines that sound more natural to the ear. There are many ways to create variation, either by using the following different types of rhyme, or by alternating the parts of speech at the end of lines, or by such techniques as *enjambment* (discussed in the exercises following). Writers often use these techniques without realizing what has created the music. After a while, these methods become second nature.

Rhyme and its variations must have meaning, just as rhythm does. A deliberate off-rhyme (defined below) among exact rhymes, for instance, might create the effect of disorder or letdown.

The following are patterns of sound and types of rhyme (defined as the repetition of the identical or similar stressed sound).

exact rhyme: differing consonant sounds followed by identical stressed vowel sounds, as in "state, gate" and "lies, surprise."

slant-rhyme: also called off-rhyme, half-rhyme, near rhyme, approximate rhyme, oblique rhyme. The sounds are similar, but not exactly alike. In the most common type of slant rhyme, the final consonant sounds are identical, but the stressed vowel sounds differ. This effect might exist at the end or in the middle of a line and is referred to as **consonance**, as in "good, food" and "soot, flute" (see Shirley Geok-Lin Lim's "Pantoum for Chinese Women" in Part Three).

assonance: the repetition, in proximity, of identical vowel sounds, preceded and followed by differing consonant sounds, as in "ten, them" and "time, mine" (see my poem, *Memento Mori in Middle School* in Part Three).

alliteration: the repetition of initial consonant sounds, as in "baby boy," or sometimes the prominent repetition of the first consonant, as in "*after* life's *final*."

masculine rhyme: also known as single rhyme. The final syllables are stressed and, after their initial consonant sounds, are identical in sound, as in "spent, meant, intent" (see Elizabeth Bishop's "One Art", among many examples).

feminine rhyme: also known as double rhyme. Stressed rhymed syllables are followed by identical unstressed syllables, as in "master, disaster, fluster" (see "One Art"), "despising, arising" (see Shakespeare's "When in Disgrace with Fortune and Men's Eyes" in Part Three).

triple rhyme: a form of feminine rhyme in which identical stressed vowel sounds are followed by two identical unstressed syllables, as in "goddesses, bodices, Odysseys" and "apology, mythology." This type of rhyme works well occasionally, but it has the greatest likelihood of slipping into light verse. It might be best employed in deliberately humorous verse (see the excerpt from Byron's *Don Juan* in the "Stanzas" chapter).

eye-rhyme: the sounds do not rhyme, but the words look as if they would rhyme, as in "rough, bough"

end rhyme: also known as terminal rhyme, the rhymes that appear at the end of lines.

internal rhyme: rhyme that appears within the line, as in "Stack to Stack / and the built hayrack back" in Donald Hall's "Names of Horses" (included in Part Three), where the rhymes in quick succession create the effect of the horses' machine-like tasks.

Two important cautions, to avoid the most common failures of rhyme in contemporary verse: First, don't go for the easiest rhyme. Rhyme should surprise. Second, don't use awkward syntax just to squeeze in a rhyme. Trying to force something to fit didn't work for Cinderella's stepsisters. Or, to reference another tale, if you force a rhyme, it will beat like a tell-tale heart in the center of your poem.

Suggestions for Writing

1. Write lines practicing each of the above elements of rhyme (exact rhyme, slant rhyme, etc.).

2. Running one line into the next, or *enjambment* (also discussed in "Hearing the Beat: Using Meter"), rather than using end-stopped lines, can enhance the flow and keep rhymes from sounding too lockstep. Notice the enjambment in Rhina P. Espaillat's "Bilingual/Bilingüe" below. Practice using enjambment to soften the sound of exact rhymes.

3. Another way to keep rhyme fresh and interesting (exact rhyme, in particular) is to vary your choice of parts of speech for the rhyming word. Write some lines that vary the parts of speech. End your lines with a verb, then a noun, then an adjective, etc., as in the example below by Rhina P. Espaillat. (Also see Espaillat's essay "Bilingual/Bilingüe" in Part Three.)

My father liked them separate, one there,	(adverb)
one here (allá y aquí), as if aware	(adjective)
that words might cut in two his daughter's heart	(noun)
(el corazón) and lock the alien part	(noun)
to what he was—his memory, his name	(noun)
(su nombre)—with a key he could not claim.	(verb)
"English outside this door, Spanish inside,"	(preposition)
he said, "y basta." But who can divide	(verb)
the world, the word (mundo y palabra) from	(preposition)
any child? I knew how to be dumb	(adjective)
and stubborn (testaruda); late, in bed,	(noun)
I hoarded secret syllables I read	(verb)

Until my tongue (mi lengua) learned to run   (verb)
where his stumbled. And still the heart was one. (noun)

I like to think he knew that, even when,   (conjunction)
proud (orgulloso) of his daughter's pen,   (noun)

he stood outside mis versos, half in fear   (noun)
of words he loved but wanted not to hear.   (verb)

22
Forms from Various Cultures and Traditions

The following pages present examples of several specific *fixed*, or closed, poetic forms:

Sonnet

Forms of repetition: sestina, villanelle, rondeau, triolet, pantoum, ghazal

Occasionals: ode, homage, elegy

Short forms: epigrams, haiku, tanka, renga

Ballad and ballade

Light verse: limerick, clerihew, double dactyl

Acrostic

Blues poetry

Prose poetry

Practicing each form is an exercise in itself, because of the framework the rules for the form provide. You will find that following these rules can actually be quite liberating—it can often bring you to a place in your stream of consciousness that you might not otherwise have found. Structure, in a way, can enable freedom, just as grammar allows us to communicate. Attempting these exercises will also shed light on great poems of history written in these forms. And being familiar with them gives you additional tools for your own writing. Writing a villanelle or triolet, for instance, can hone the skill of using a repeated line or refrain. Once you have a good grasp of the form, you can use its influence to your best advantage—either by using the form itself or using it as inspiration for your own variations. When you find a form that particularly suits or intrigues you, search out its more elaborate history and the many examples in literature.

Working in form can help to train your ear and can have the effect of making your free verse and prose more lyrical and rhythmical. It is also vital to note, however, that a competent exercise in a particular form is not necessarily a great poem. As I have mentioned several times in the book, we must keep in mind that the source of true art remains on many levels an enigma.

Remember, also, that it may take a while for a subject to discover its true shape. Form should have meaning and purpose in a particular piece and find its subject organically. Writers spend decades, sometimes, working on a single short poem. It is a good idea to think of much of your writing as "exercise." It takes the pressure off, opens up the field to many possibilities, and keeps you going.

Sonnet

Read/Revisit

Marilyn Nelson, "Chosen" (see page 200)
William Shakespeare, "When in Disgrace with Fortune and Men's Eyes" (see page 207)
R. S. Gwynn, "Shakespearean Sonnet" (see page 181)

The sonnet is a fourteen-line poem and one of the most well-known verse forms. The word *sonnet* comes from the Italian *sonetto*, meaning "a little song or sound," which previously came from the Latin *sonus*, meaning "sound." The sonnet form is thought to have been invented by Giacomo de Lentino around the year 1200.

Many traditional sonnets were written in iambic pentameter: five feet or ten syllables to every line, with every other syllable stressed. There are different traditional rhyme schemes for the sonnet, the best known being the following:

Shakespeare: abab cdcd efef gg
Spenser: ababbcbccdcdee
Petrarch: abba abba with the sestet rhyming either cdcdcd, cdecde, cdccdc, or some other variation that doesn't end in a couplet
Wordsworth: abbaacca dedeff

The first eight lines or *octave* of the Petrarchan sonnet presents the theme and develops it. In the following *sestet*, the first three lines reflect upon the theme and the final three lines bring it to a close. The Shakespearean sonnet allows a break between octave and sestet but is generally composed of three quatrains, each with different pairs of rhymes, and a final couplet with its own rhyme. An important feature of the Shakespearean sonnet is this last couplet, which closes the poem with a climax, or a philosophical reflection on what has been presented. Spenser's form has an octave followed by a sestet that includes a final couplet. Many other poets, such as Milton and Wordsworth, have developed other variations of the sonnet.

Sonnets are sometimes written in a *sequence* or cycle. Some of these cycles (such as a crown or garland of sonnets) have a particular number and elaborate structure. The *garland* of sonnets used by several Russian poets, for instance, consists of fifteen poems. They are arranged so that the final sonnet contains only lines repeated from the preceding poems.

Considering the many sonnets written by such poets as Yeats, Frost, Millay, Nelson, and Gwynn, to name just a few, one can see that the form has thrived into modern and contemporary work. Many contemporary sonnets are written with nontraditional meters and rhyme schemes, or without rhyme, and contain a variety of subjects.

Marilyn Nelson's "Chosen" uses both exact and slant rhyme and shapes the sonnet into tercets and a concluding couplet. She uses the form's compression to articulate a terrible incident that has a historical weight. Consider how Nelson's "Chosen" and Gwynn's "Shakespearean Sonnet" both use tradition and bend it, in both the form and choice of subjects.

Suggestions for Writing

1. Try the sonnet. You could select a rhyme scheme. Or, as you write the first few lines, a rhyme scheme may begin to emerge. To better understand the form, I encourage you to use iambic pentameter (with minimal variations) at first. (See "Hearing the Beat: Using Meter.") Later, you can experiment with more variations. Though the subject of love often conjures up a sonnet, don't feel limited to this. Consider the startling subjects of Gwynn's and Nelson's contemporary sonnets. Perhaps use the compression of a sonnet to depict a traumatic event, as Marilyn Nelson does. Note, also, Nelson's use of paradox (or contradiction) to deal with the terror.

2. "Translate" Shakespeare's sonnet into a love poem in contemporary English or, perhaps, a different character's voice.

Forms of Repetition: Sestina, Villanelle, Rondeau, Triolet, Pantoum, Ghazal

Sestina

Read/Revisit

Dana Gioia, "My Confessional Sestina" (see page 179)

The word *sestina* comes from the Italian *sesto*, meaning "sixth" (from the Latin root *sextus*). This form is based on sixes and is an ideal exercise for the mathematical mind. The elaborate repetitions are reminiscent of the patterns we see in the natural world. The form is thought to have been invented in Provence in the thirteenth century by the troubadour poet Arnaut Daniel. Dante admired Daniel's poetry and popularized the form by writing sestinas in Italian.

The sestina has six unrhymed stanzas of six lines each, with the end words repeating in a precise pattern throughout the poem. The repeated words create a rhyme-like effect that occurs at seemingly unpredictable intervals as the pattern changes from stanza to stanza. The poem then ends with a three-line stanza, each line containing two of the words. The pattern would be as follows, with the capital letters representing end words:

ABCDEF / FAEBDC / CFDABE / ECBFAD / DEACFB / BDFECA / AB,CD,EF

The final poem therefore contains thirty-nine lines made up of 6 + 6 + 6 + 6 + 6 + 6 + 3.

When used to the poem's advantage, the repetitions create a forward movement, and the words serve different functions in the progression of the poem. They might also create a cyclical effect.

Many poets have enjoyed working in the sestina form, including Algernon Charles Swinburne, Rudyard Kipling, Ezra Pound, Elizabeth Bishop, W. H. Auden, Donald Justice, and Mona Van Duyn. Dana Gioia's "My Confessional Sestina" uses the form to make a satirical comment about workshop poems, as well as confessional poetry.

Suggestions for Writing

1. In a workshop (ignoring Gioia's wry comment on the workshop sestina for the moment), to make sense of the form, you might work with a group to write a collective sestina. Choose six words and write them on the board. Set up a grid for the poem. Have participants call out lines that end with the appropriate words.

Don't expect an exquisite poem to emerge, but it is a fun way to make sense of the form, and some interesting lines will likely appear.

2. Though it may be easy to follow the rules and "fill in the blanks" to create a passable sestina, writing a good one is not an easy task. It is definitely not the form for all subjects. Sestinas tend to lag midway, and a good one needs a serious charge or turn of events, perhaps a narrative twist. Try to choose a subject that will have some shift at its center. Another hint is to change the grammar of the chosen words, as in Gioia's use of "taste."

3. Adopt (and adapt) six words from a writer who has influenced you. Give credit to your source. Use them to write an "homage," perhaps. Donald Justice did this in his "Sestina on Six Words by Weldon Kees."

4. Since so many sestinas seem to lag, the form might provide a good opportunity to invent a new form. Use the concept and pattern of repetition, but try a half sestina, a *sestria*, perhaps.

5. As Gioia does, make a comment about a particular form while using the form. Many writers have done this. Louise Bogan, for instance, in "Single Sonnet," chooses the form of a sonnet to address the "heroic mould" of the sonnet.

Villanelle

Read/Revisit

> Elizabeth Bishop, "One Art" (see page 161)
> Wendy Cope, "Lonely Hearts" (see page 167)

The word *villanelle* comes from *villanella*—a type of old Italian folk song. The villanelle contains six stanzas: five stanzas of three lines and one stanza of four lines. The first and last lines of the first stanza are repeated throughout the poem in the intricate pattern of A^1bA^2 / abA^1 / abA^2 / abA^1 / abA^2 / abA^1A^2. (The capitals refer to *repeated* lines and the lower case letters to *rhymes* with the repeated lines. The numbers 1 and 2 refer to the two lines that repeat precisely.) The poem has a rhyme scheme of aba throughout, with a variation in the last stanza.

The pattern of repetition in the villanelle can create a cyclical, hypnotic effect, like a tide coming back in. The form also reinforces the ideas expressed in the poem.

Elizabeth Bishop's "One Art" is a powerful example of the possibilities of the villanelle. In this poem, she is talking about loss, and the poem moves through the different kinds of loss one might experience. The subject is a good one for this form, in which the repetition has a deliberate function. Notice that she does not repeat the A^2 line exactly, but she repeats its meaning. She also alters the A^1 line in the last stanza. The variation is enchanting.

The villanelle can also be an appropriate form to convey an element of humor or irony. Wendy Cope's "Lonely Hearts" uses the villanelle to explore the personal ads, which seem more and more a reality of modern life. The form in this poem enhances the subject. The repetition has a distinct purpose here, as does the rhyme. Otherwise, the poem might read as a mere series of ads.

The villanelle form is a good one as an exercise because it helps to hone the skill of using a repeated line, like the refrain of a song. In a case such as "One Art," it might allow one to explore the many layers that surround a single subject, such as loss. In "Lonely Hearts," the repetition achieves the "listing" effect of newspaper ads, and provides a humorous commentary on how similar all the ads tend to sound.

Other contemporary poets have found the villanelle useful for conveying various subjects. Carolyn Beard Whitlow, for instance, has used the villanelle as a blues poem, another form with a structure of repetition. (See the "Blues Poetry" section, later in Part Two.)

Suggestions for Writing

Try writing a villanelle. You might choose a subject that has many angles to explore, so the repetition has a purpose and does not become tedious. Allow the form to work for you. Try to create movement within the poem by exploring different layers of meaning in the repeated line or by creating a narrative within.

Rondeau and Triolet

Read/Revisit

Paul Laurence Dunbar, "We Wear the Mask" (see page 169)
Gerry Cambridge "Goldfinch in Spring" (see page 164)
Frederick Morgan, "1904" (see page 199)

The word *rondeau* comes from the French *rond*, meaning "round," as each line comes round, or is repeated. The rondeau consists of thirteen lines divided into three stanzas. The first and last stanzas contain five lines, and the second stanza contains three lines (not including the refrains). There are two rhymes in the poem. The opening words of the first line (or sometimes the whole first line) form unrhymed refrains in the second and third stanzas, often puns. The pattern is aabba, aabR, aabbaR. (The R signifies the refrain.)

The *triolet*, essentially a shorter version of the rondeau, was popular among French medieval poets such as Eustace Deschamps. It was revived by Jean de la Fontaine in the seventeenth century and remained popular into the nineteenth century.

The triolet is another form particularly useful for subjects that contain several angles or layers, or a cyclical quality. Frederick Morgan's "1904" is a good variation on the form, where the single repetition enhances the idea of a secret kept for years.

Suggestions for Writing

Try a triolet or rondeau. Choose a subject that might benefit from the reinforcement of a line, like the cycles felt (or heard) in contemporary Scottish poet Gerry Cambridge's poem, "Goldfinch in Spring" or the passage of time in Frederick Morgan's poem, "1904." In Cambridge's poem, note also the effect of the varying grammar of each line.

Get a handle on each form by trying to adhere to it first. Later, you can experiment with variations, and use the repetition to its greatest advantage in your particular poem.

Pantoum

Read/Revisit

Shirley Geok-Lin Lim, "Pantoum for Chinese Women" (see page 193)

The *pantoum*, of Malaysian origin, is another form using repetition. Victor Hugo first described the pantoum in the West. It became a popular form (with some variations) among French poets such as Louisa Siefert and Charles Baudelaire. It became prevalent in England in the late nineteenth century but was not used much in America until the last half of the twentieth century.

The poem is made up of four-line stanzas: lines two and four of one stanza are repeated as lines one and three of the next. The poem can have any length. Sometimes the final stanza uses the first and third lines of the first stanza as its second and fourth lines. This creates the effect of completion, giving the poem a feeling of having come full circle.

Shirley Geok-Lin Lim's "Pantoum for Chinese Women" (included in Part Three) takes on the heavy subject of Chinese female infanticide as a result of the one-child law. The "soot" in the poem refers to a common method of smothering girl children. Of her choice of form for this poem, Lim has stated that she believes poetry must give pleasure and that use of meter and rhyme are ways to enhance the musicality. She believes that sometimes the most terrible subjects might best be cast in language that gives the most pleasure, as if to somehow rise beyond the horror.

Suggestions for Writing

As a pantoum can be of any length, start with a few stanzas. Be willing to change your initial lines if you find yourself heading in a different direction than you intended—which often happens with such a form.

Ghazal

The *ghazal* (pronounced *ghuzzle*, with the *gh* in the throat like the French *r*) is an ancient Persian form. Hafiz (1325–1389) is considered the master of the ghazal, although many Persian poets, such as Rumi, Jami, and Sanai, also composed many ghazals. Ghalib (1797–1869) is generally considered the master of the form in Urdu (the youngest of the many languages of India).

The ghazal contains a series of couplets. Each couplet ends with the same word or set of words. The couplets should each stand alone (almost like haiku, perhaps) but are also connected by the leap the mind takes via the disunity. Although the ghazal receives its name from a word that means "sweet talk," or talk for a beloved, the loved one is often a mystical beloved. The couplets often contain an element of longing.

The traditional Persian form of the ghazal had a precise metrical and rhyming structure, but the meter does not have an English equivalent. The opening couplet (*matla*) rhymes and sets up the structure for the poem—the rhyme scheme (*qafi*) and the refrain (*radif*). To best approximate the traditional Persian form, each of the lines should contain the same number of syllables, although some poets operate on a principle of accents per line, rather than syllable count.

According to Vinod Sena of Delhi University, the term also derives from the same root as the word *gazelle*. Sena likens the couplet of the ghazal to the final couplet of the Shakespearean sonnet:

> Just as a deer in the forest bounds from place to place, likewise the form of lyric poetry known as the ghazal is expected to have that same bounce. . . . So it bounds from one verse to another, and each such verse or couplet is a world of meaning unto itself. . . . The Shakespearean couplet seems to sum up the essence of whatever has gone before in a Shakespearean sonnet. Imagine a series of such couplets with that same intensity and completeness of meaning in each making up a single poem. Nine such verses would be like nine Shakespearean sonnets compressed into nine couplets.

The ghazal form first became known in Europe in the early 1800s with a German translation of Hafiz. Goethe modeled Hafiz in his *West-Eastern Divan*. The following translation of one of Hafiz's many ghazals does not have a consistent syllable count, but it does show the pattern of repetition at the end of each couplet. Certain images appear often in traditional ghazals, such as wine, tears, the cup, the cup-bearer, the tavern, the beloved. The many symbols of intoxication refer to the intoxication of love or grace. One of the elements of the form is its use of this tradition of images in new patterns. Each image may have many meanings. Much may be lost in translation, however, as only one sense of a word is often conveyed.

> If from the rock in Badakhshan, the ruby will come forth.
> From the mountain gorge, like sugar, the water of the Rukni will
>   come forth.

Within the city of Shiraz, from the door of every house,
A heart-ravisher, lovely, graceful, will come forth.

From the dwelling of the kazi, of the mufti, of the shaikh, and of
the muhtasib,
Unalloyed wine, rose of hue, will come forth.

On the pulpit, at the time of ecstasy, and of the manifestation
of hypocrisy,
From the top of the admonisher's turban, "bang," will come forth.

Within the garden, morn and eve, with the voice of the minstrel,
The lament of the bulbul with the twang of the harp will come
forth.

In such a city (of love's tumult), in separation from the beloved,
and in grief for separation,
From his dwelling, (O wonder) Hafiz, straight of heart, will come
forth.

HAFIZ (C. 1320–C.1390); TRANS. H. WILBERFORCE CLARKE

The ghazal sometimes contains a *makhta* (signature couplet with the poet's name) as the final couplet, as in Hafiz's example above. This signature might take many forms. Agha Shahid Ali, for instance, chooses to use the makhta to define his name "Shahid":

Listen: it means "The Beloved" in Persian, "witness" in Arabic.

AGHA SHAHID ALI (1949–2003)

John Hollander, in *Rhyme's Reason: A Guide to English Verse*, uses the traditional pattern of the ghazal in a poem that clarifies the requirements for the traditional form quite well:

For couplets the ghazal is prime; at the end
Of each one's a refrain like a chime: "at the end."

Hollander closes his ghazal with a signature but gives himself the pseudonym *Qafia Radif*, the terms for the rhyme scheme and refrain of a ghazal:

Now Qafia Radif has grown weary, like life,
At the game he's been wasting his time at. THE END.

JOHN HOLLANDER (B. 1929)

Although some poets have written unrhymed ghazals, others such as Agha Shahid Ali encourage a more faithful return to the traditional form of the poem, in order to create the unity within the disunity. Ali comments that "because of Urdu's quantitative syllables and meters, a ghazal usually seems to have the same number of syllables per line when recited or sung." However, one might choose to vary the syllable count and choice of meter. Hollander, for instance, uses mostly anapestic meter but occasionally varies it with iambic meter (see "Hearing the Beat: Using Meter").

At a *mushaira*, a Persian poetry gathering, when the poet recites the first line, sometimes his listeners will recite it back. There is a call and response (see "Blues Poetry") inherent in the poem's structure as well as in the musicality of its rhyme scheme and repetition. The refrain sets up an expectation for the listener and an excitement to hear how the next couplet will use the final words. Listeners will sometimes break into the known refrain before the couplet is completed.

Suggestions for Writing

1. Try writing an unrhymed ghazal as well as the traditional form of the ghazal, using the rhyme and refrain.

2. To spark your mind, you might use the results from the "random" exercises in the "Random Connections" section in Part One. Note how the series of "if-then, why-because" responses (on the surface disconnected) have an undercurrent of unity.

3. In a workshop, you could write a communal ghazal. Write the first couplet as a group. Decide on a pattern, and then each person writes a couplet. Read the couplets out loud—as a single ghazal.

4. In a workshop, read ghazals aloud, with audience participation, in the tradition of the mushaira.

Occasionals: Ode, Homage, Elegy

Read/Revisit

> John Keats, "Ode on a Grecian Urn" (see page 189)
> Donald Hall, "Names of Horses" (see page 182)
> César Vallejo, "To My Brother Miguel" (see page 215)

The ode, homage, and elegy are often written for a particular occasion or in honor of someone or something.

Ode

The *ode* (from the Greek word *aeidein*, "to sing") has undergone many changes throughout history—from the Greek poet Pindar's victory odes to the Horatian odes, such as those of Alexander Pope—to irregular odes, such as Keats's "Ode on a Grecian Urn." The ode is generally considered a lyric poem that addresses someone or something not present. Today, the ode is often used to address a variety of people and everday objects, as in Pablo Neruda's surprising subject in "Ode to a Watermelon."

Homage

Many poets have written poems as an *homage*, or expression of respect, to someone or something, in particular in homage to other poets. Several of Donald Justice's poems declare an influence in the very title: "After a Phrase Abandoned by Wallace Stevens," "Homage to the Memory of Wallace Stevens," "Variations on a Text by Vallejo," or "Sestina on Six Words by Weldon Kees."

Contemporary writers have also used the homage for a variety of unexpected and somewhat irrelevant topics. Lucille Clifton, for instance, often opens her poetry readings with a poem about her own body. "Homage to My Hips." The poem is humorous and playful, with the hips having a will of their own and even magic qualities, but also has a serious undercurrent in lines such as "these hips have never been enslaved." It certainly expands the traditional notion of homage.

Elegy

The *elegy* is also an ancient form, the word deriving from the Greek word *elegeia* (song of mourning). The elegy in ancient Greek and Latin was not always "elegiac" in the modern sense. It was any poem in the elegiac meter, which consists of a *distich*, or couplet, with one line of classical hexameter (dactylic, six beats) and the second of elegiac pentameter (five beats), as in the following lines from "Pasa Thalassa Thalassa," by Edwin Arlington Robinson:

> Down with a twittering flash go the smooth and inscrutable
>   swallows,
> Down to the place made theirs by the cold work of the sea.
> EDWIN ARLINGTON ROBINSON (1869–1945)

In English, the traditional elegiac stanza is a four-line stanza of iambic pentameter, rhymed abab. However, the elegy has taken on many different forms throughout time and geography.

Among the Romans in the first century, the elegy was mostly used for love poems. John Donne returned to the origins of the form with his funeral elegy, as did German poets Johann Wolfgang Goethe and Friedrich Schiller. American poet Walt Whitman's famous long elegy "When Lilacs Last in the Dooryard Bloom'd" is both a lament and a coming to terms, following the Civil War. German poet Rainer Maria Rilke wrote his famous "Duino Elegies" in 1912, ten poems that reflect on art and death.

Clearly, the elegy can have a variety of forms and subjects. César Vallejo writes an elegy for his brother Miguel and the "extinguished afternoons" of their youth together. Donald Hall's "Names of Horses" also has an elegiac nature, addressing the horses of our history, the burdens they carried, and their often ignoble deaths.

Suggestions for Writing

1. Try writing an ode, homage, or elegy, depending on which meets the present conditions of your life.

2. For the ode, try addressing a piece of art, as Keats does in "Ode on a Grecian Urn." In a workshop, bring in a photograph of the piece of art you are addressing. You might also find and bring in a photograph of a Grecian urn (sometimes you can find translations of their distinctive inscriptions) to give an idea of the kind of art that inspired Keats's poem. (See "Writing from Art" in Part One.)

3. For the ode or homage, perhaps take a lead from Pablo Neruda's "Ode to the Watermelon" or Lucille Clifton's "Homage to My Hips" and choose an everyday object.

4. Write an homage to a writer who has influenced you. Reflect on a line or idea that has always remained with you. Declare your source of inspiration in the title, within the piece, or as an epigraph perhaps.

5. An elegy might be an occasion for reflection on a recent or not-so-recent loss. Consider the way Hall addresses the horses in "Names of Horses." Write an elegy for something nonhuman that has been lost, perhaps directly addressing the animal, plant, idea, etc.

Short Forms: Epigram, Haiku, Tanka, Renga

Epigram

The epigram is a short, often witty poem, meant to be remembered. The word *epigram* derives from the Greek word meaning "write on," as on a gravestone or a wall, for instance. Such writing tended to be brief, given the limited space, not to mention the labor of carving each letter in stone. Epigrams have survived from antiquity in many languages (probably because they were carved in stone) and convey such subjects as history, irony, and love. The following is a translation of an early Persian poet:

> I'll hide within my poems as I write them
> Hoping to kiss your lips as you recite them.
> AMAREH (11TH CENTURY); TRANS. DICK DAVIS

An epigram need not rhyme or follow a particular meter, although very many do, given the nature of the form as one to be remembered. Rhyme certainly enhances that intention.

> Sir, I admit your general rule,
> That every poet is a fool:
> But you yourself may serve to show it,
> That every fool is not a poet.
> ALEXANDER POPE (1688–1744)

> John, while swimming in the ocean,
> rubbed sharks' backs with suntan lotion.
> Now the sharks have skin of bronze
> in their bellies, namely John's.
> X. J. KENNEDY (B. 1929)

> Adam
> Had 'em
> ANONYMOUS

Haiku, Tanka, Renga

Japanese forms have also found their way into English poetry. For over a thousand years, tanka have been written: five-line poems with thirty-one syllables, following the pattern 5, 7, 5, 7, 7. The popular *haiku* (which means "beginning verse" in Japanese) derives from the first lines of tanka. The haiku (or hokku), a poem of seventeen syllables (5, 7, 5), often depicts something in nature, but it carries in its compressed style a mystical suggestion of other interpretations. It is important to note, however, that the Japanese syllable is quite a different entity than the English syllable. Therefore, an English haiku need not necessarily have seventeen syllables, but rather three short lines. The poem might have one of many tones, from somber to humorous. The most important thing is the leap contained in the poem's compression. The poem should reverberate.

> Under cherry trees
> Soup, the salad, fish, and all . . .
> Seasoned with petals.
>
> Matsuo Basho (1644–1694)

> Cricket, watch
> out! I'm rolling
> over!
>
> Kobayashi Issa (1763–1827)

Haiku were also used as the first three lines for a series of tanka called *renga*. Renga were often collaborative poems, and many Japanese poets wrote books of rules for the form. Each stanza would connect to the previous one (through an image, perhaps, or a play on words), but not to the stanza before. The rules would also describe the pacing from beginning to end. The first six or eight stanzas would set up the poem. The middle stanzas would become quite elaborate, include humor, and move through a great range of subjects and emotions. The final six or eight stanzas would move quickly, with rapid, closely related images, like simple farewells at the end of a gathering. Often the final stanza would contain an image of spring, indicating hope and rejuvenation. Traditionally, Japanese renga might involve over two hundred poets writing a single poem.

Matsuo Basho, considered one of the great writers of haiku, preferred renga of thirty-six stanzas. He spoke of the linking technique as having the essential quality of *hibiki*, or echo. He believed that the second stanza should echo the first, via a thread of connection, as in the following (the poem need not rhyme, of course, although the following translation does):

From this day on,
I will be known as a wanderer
leaving in morning showers.

You will sleep your nights
Nestled among *sasanqua* flowers.

MATSUO BASHO (1644–1694); TRANS. DIANE THIEL

Basho is known also for his travelogues—which were written as a mosaic of prose and poetry, and which often contained linked poems, the parts often identified as "written by host" or "written by guest," a kind of call and response.

Japanese forms have been much revived in contemporary verse and have often been used in innovative ways. W. H. Auden's "Elegy for JFK," for instance, is formally intriguing in its use of a series of haiku. And many poets, such as Mexican poet Octavio Paz, have revived the tradition of collaborative renga, with one poet producing the first three lines and another poet the following two.

Suggestions for Writing

1. Try writing an epigram. Choose a subject that would benefit from getting right to the point. Make a statement about love. Give advice. Use irony. One common type of epigram presents the poet pretending to be something inanimate and is often a riddle.

2. Try writing haiku and tanka. In a group setting, you might revive the ancient tradition of renga and attempt poems in collaboration. The first person would write the first stanza of three lines, the second person would write the next stanza of two lines, the third person would write the following stanza, again of three lines, as discussed above.

3. Just for fun, you might try the types of links discussed in the exercises in "Random Connections," in Part One, to see what kind of accidental connections arise. Write your tanka (or haiku) individually, but read them as if they were a renga written in collaboration. See what mysterious echoes appear.

Ballad and Ballade

Read/Revisit

Nikos Kavadias, "A Knife" (see page 188)
Dudley Randall, "Ballad of Birmingham" (see page 204)

Both the ballad and the ballade express the tradition of the link between poetry, story, and song, although they are rather different forms.

Ballade

The *ballade* is a French form. Some of the greatest inventors of form were the troubadour poets of southern France, who flourished between the eleventh and thirteenth centuries. The poets sought patrons among the nobility, although occasionally members of the nobility, for instance, Richard the Lion-Hearted, were troubadours themselves. Troubadours would often travel with apprentices or *jongleurs*, who would accompany the poems with music.

The ballade (from an old French word meaning "dancing song") was a popular troubadour form, usually following a pattern of three stanzas of eight lines each. The form continued to be popular in fourteenth- and fifteenth-century France, with such poets as Charles d'Orleans, Christine de Pisan, and François Villon. The rhyme scheme is ababbcbC. (The capital C denotes a line that is repeated at the end of each of the three stanzas.) The whole poem follows the pattern of ababbcbC ababbcbC ababbcbC bcbC. There are some variations on the form. The stanza has sometimes consisted of ten lines, where a D would be added. The ballade has often been addressed to a specific person or was written for a particular occasion. It has not been used very widely in English, possibly due to the intricate rhyme scheme, although some poets found the form appropriate for certain subjects.

Geoffrey Chaucer (considered the first great poet of English), poor in his old age, sent the following ballade to his new king, Henry IV, entreating more funds. The king must have appreciated the poem, as he raised Chaucer's pension soon after. "The Complaint of Chaucer to His Purse" is written in middle English but, with a few words clarified, can be readily understood, as can the somewhat exaggerated lament for more money.

To yow, my purse, and to noon other wight°	*person*
Complayne I, for ye be my lady dere!	
I am so sory, now that ye be lyght;	
For certes,° but° ye make me heavy chere,	*surely / unless*
Me were as leef° be layd upon my bere;	*I would like to be*

For which unto your mercy thus I crye:
Beth hevy ageyn, or elles moote° I dye!   *must*

Now voucheth sauf° this day, or° yt be nyght,   *vouchsafe / before*
That I of yow the blisful soun° may here,   *sound*
Or see your colour lyk the sonne bryght,
That of yelownesse hadde never pere.
Ye be my lyf, ye be myn hertes stere,°   *guide*
Quene of comfort and of good companye:
Beth hevy ageyn, or elles moote I dye!

Now purse, that ben to me my lyves lyght
And saveour, as° doun in this world here,   *while*
Out of this toune helpe me thurgh your myght,
Syn that ye wole nat ben my tresorere;
For I am shave as nye° as any frere.°   *close / friar*
But yet I pray unto your curtesye:
Beth heavy ageyn, or elles moote I dye!   *L'envoy de Chaucer:*
O conqueror of Brutes° Albyon,°   *Brutus's England*
Which that by lyne and free eleccion
Been verray° kyng, this song to yow I sende; *true*
And ye, that mowen° alle our harmes amende, *can*
Have mynde upon my supplicacion!

GEOFFREY CHAUCER (C. 1340–1400)

Ballad

The ballad has been traditionally used for the purpose of story-telling and has quite a different basic structure from the ballade. Any narrative song might be called a ballad. Traditionally, ballads would shift and change as they traveled from place to place. Sir Walter Scott, a renowned collector of Scottish folk ballads, angered a few of his sources by the act. One woman said to him, "They were made for singing and no' for reading, but ye ha'e broken the charm now and they'll never be sung mair." Perhaps something of the oral tradition does get lost in the act of transcribing a ballad—it freezes it in time. On the other hand, the transcribers of ballads and other forms of folklore certainly preserved much of our culture that would have otherwise been lost.

Ballad meter varies, but the traditional ballad stanza is four lines rhymed abcb or abab, with alternating beats of 4, 3, 4, 3. If the feet are iambic, the quatrain is said to have *common measure*, as in eighteenth-century English hymnist John Newton's "Amazing Grace:"

Amazing grace! how sweet the sound
    That saved a wretch like me!
I once was lost, but now am found,
    Was blind, but now I see.

The ballad has often been used as a form to convey historical events, and it has been adopted by contemporary writers for this purpose. Consider Dudley Randall's "Ballad of Birmingham," for instance (the poem is included in Part Three). The subject matter of ballads ranges from the comic and irreverent to very serious and poignant depictions of events, as in Kavadias's and Randall's poems.

Suggestions for Writing

1. Ballad scholar Albert B. Friedman has said that the events of ballads are frequently "the stuff of tabloid journalism—sensational tales of lust, revenge and domestic crime." Use a tabloid newspaper to select subjects for your ballads. (In all honesty, you could probably use any newspaper, considering the nature of much of today's sensationalism in the everyday news.)

2. The subject matter of Chaucer's hyperbolic ballade transcends time and almost asks to be spoofed. Write a modern imitation of the poem, requesting money from parents, a boss, a governmental organization, etc. (For other suggestions for modernizations, see the exercise with Shakespeare in the "Sonnet" section and with Poe in the "Tell-Tale Dialect" section of the chapter on "Diction.")

3. Note how both Randall's ballad and Kavadias's ballad have more than one voice. Try writing a narrative poem for more than one voice.

Light Verse: Limerick, Clerihew, Double Dactyl

The limerick, clerihew, and double dactyl forms usually contain light verse. We are all familiar with the *limerick*, made popular by Edward Lear. The form contains three long and two short lines rhyming aabba and usually has a bawdy subject. The rhymes are often more aural than visual, as in "pursued her" and "barracuda" in the following:

> There was a young man from Tahiti
> who went for a swim with his sweetie,
> and as he pursued her,
> a blind barracuda
> ran off with his masculinity.
>
> Anonymous

The following example describes the form and its limits quite well:

> A limerick packs laughs anatomical
> Into space that is quite economical.
>   But the good ones I've seen
>   So seldom are clean,
> And the clean ones so seldom are comical.
>
> Anonymous

The *clerihew*, invented by Edmund Clerihew Bentley (1875–1956), contains two mismatched couplets, one of which contains the name and element of biography of someone as one of the rhymes. At a recent writing conference, R. S. Gwynn immortalized a large percentage of conference participants by writing clerihews with their names. He assumed the *nom de plume* Clara Hughes for the act. A favorite was the clerihew he wrote for poet David Mason, using the aural joke of rhyming "naiad" with Gwynn's southern drawl of "bad":

> David Mason
> was last seen chason
> an Aegean naiad.
> He's so bad.
>
> R. S. Gwynn (b. 1948)

The *double dactyl* was originated by poet Anthony Hecht (b. 1923). The form has two quatrains, with the last lines of each rhyming. The first three lines of each quatrain have two full dactyls. (A dactyl is one stressed syllable followed by two unstressed syllables—see the "Hearing the Beat: Using Meter" chapter.) The last line of each quatrain has a meter of stressed, unstressed, unstressed, stressed. Somewhere in the poem, usually in the sixth line, there has to be a single double-dactyl word, such as "gubernatorial" or "incomprehensible":

Tact

Patty-cake, patty-cake
Marcus Antonius,
What do you think of the
African Queen?
Gubernatorial
Duties require my
Presence in Egypt. Ya
Know what I mean?

PAUL PASCAL (B. 1925)

Suggestions for Writing

Trying your hand at limericks, clerihews, and double dactyls can be great fun as well as a good challenge. Given the right subject and touch, each of these forms might even rise above the name of light verse. Or rather, give light verse a better name.

Acrostic

Read/Revisit

David Mason, "Acrostic from Aegina" (see page 196)

The *acrostic* originated in ancient times. Some of the Hebrew psalms of the Bible are acrostics. The word derives from the Greek *acros* (outermost) and *stichos* (line of poetry). In an acrostic, the letters of the lines spell a vertical word, or group of words. A double acrostic has two vertical arrangements in the middle or at the end of the line. And a (rare) triple acrostic has three vertical arrangements.

The acrostic has been enjoyed over time as a game—from the Greeks to Boccaccio to Chaucer to Edgar Allan Poe. In its design, the acrostic often contains a secret or riddle. It might carry the name of a beloved, as in David Mason's "Acrostic from Aegina."

With its hidden word or message, the acrostic can have a subversive quality. Mason names his poem as an acrostic, but sometimes the acrostic is concealed. *The New Yorker*, for instance, once unknowingly published an acrostic that named and insulted a prominent anthologist. (There is, in fact, a tradition of the insult poem, which makes use of humor and exaggeration and often contains an element of "call and response," as one might imagine—a trading of insults. The epigram has also been a popular form for insult poems.)

Suggestions for Writing

1. Write an acrostic that spells the name of your beloved, honors or dishonors a person in history, contains a riddle, or is an insult poem. Choose a subject that would truly benefit from the "secret message" nature of the poem.

2. Try an *abecedarian*, a variant of an acrostic. In this form, each line begins with a letter of the alphabet, in order.

Blues Poetry

Read/Revisit

Carolyn Beard Whitlow, "Rockin' a Man Stone Blind" (see page 216)
Langston Hughes, "The Weary Blues" (see page 187)

Blues poetry has its roots in music, and in the experience of African Americans. The earliest form was the work song: the call and response from one person to another working in the field. These work songs are often referred to as "field hollers." The songs were sometimes secret messages passed back and forth. Slaves were often silenced for fear of the subversive nature of their songs.

Blues poetry emerged from blues music, via such poets as Langston Hughes and Sterling Brown. Although "the blues" is traditionally associated with painful experience, it also has as its center the idea of the triumph of the human spirit.

Some blues poetry adheres to no particular form but is considered blues because of its content. Some has both the content and structure of repetition that old blues songs contain. The traditional blues stanza had three lines, with the first line repeated (with variations) in the second line, and then a third rhyming line. Some blues songs have a structure of four lines.

> In the evenin', in the evenin', momma, when the sun go down,
> In the evenin', darlin' I declare, when the sun go down,
> Yes it's so lonesome, so lonesome, when the one you love is not
>   around.
>
> TRADITIONAL

> I woke up this mornin' feelin' round for my shoes
> Know about that, I got these old walkin' blues
> I woke up this mornin' feelin' round for my shoes
> I know about that, I got them old walkin' blues
>
> ROBERT JOHNSON (1911–1938)

Some contemporary poets have used the blues tradition in innovative ways. Carolyn B. Whitlow, for instance, writes her poem "Rockin' a Man Stone Blind" in the form of a villanelle (see "Villanelle").

Many of us, when we compare our lives to conditions in other eras or geographic locations, might feel that we can't possibly be true to the blues, which emerged out of such tremendous human suffering. This kind of poem might provoke some unmasking, or some serious thought about the conditions of our lives (and possibly about our apathy). But we all have cultural and historical memory we can access.

The persistent problems of human society—war, oppression, cruelty to human beings as well as animals—can be subjects one might draw upon as inspiration for the blues. Poems about such universal conditions might have the power to open up our minds to the enduring questions about human existence.

Be true to your sorrow, or the sorrows you feel around you in the world. Singing them out can be one way of addressing them.

Suggestions for Writing

1. Write a blues poem. Try listening to blues music before you write. You might try Robert Johnson, Blind Lemon Jefferson, or Lightnin' Hopkins, to name a few. This exercise in workshops might produce some serious blues poems, or it might be a forum for participants to find out their concerns.

2. What is your deepest sorrow? There is a repeated motif in the blues tradition, of meeting the devil at the crossroads. You might write about your own such encounter, a crossroads of your own life. Try the structure of repetition.

3. Try writing a blues poem from someone else's perspective. Think of someone who has undergone something very difficult, and write from that perspective.

Prose Poetry

Read/Revisit

Carolyn Forché, "The Colonel" (see page 175)

Some poetry has no verse lines and is referred to as *prose poetry*. The term itself has caused quite a bit of controversy. What exactly are the requirements for a prose poem? One might question, for instance, if a piece is a vignette or a prose poem. Genre distinctions can be blurred, and this form, as a fusion of genres, eludes definition. In a prose poem, the line as a unit is not a consideration, as it is in other poetry. However, prose poems are usually marked by other poetic devices, such as metaphor or symbol. The attention to rhythm in a prose poem sometimes bears a close resemblance to that of lineated poetry. Prose poems often have a stream-of-consciousness quality, while simultaneously being steeped in wry humor and the details of the everyday world.

Poets have chosen the form of the prose poem for a variety of reasons, sometimes to emphasize a need for a kind of "reportage," rather than "poeticizing." Carolyn Forché chose the form for "The Colonel," a chilling piece which reflects the horrors she was made aware of in El Salvador. In an interview in the *American Poetry Review*, Forché commented, "I had only to pare down the memory and render it whole, unlined and as precise as recollection would have it. I did not wish to endanger myself by the act of poeticizing such a necessary reportage." She acknowledges this wish quite bluntly in the center of the poem when the speaker declares, "there is no other way to say this," as she describes the human ears which the Colonel spills onto the table. This declaration also renders an element of "meta-writing" to the piece, since the process of writing is evoked within the poem.

Nevertheless, Forché's piece, however "unpoeticized," does have distinct features which one might ascribe to poetry. There is an undercurrent of metrical lines within the poem, evoking perhaps the secret poetics of being witness to such horror. Repetitions of sounds in series of words such as "house," "lace," "stores," "terrace," "faces," "voice" suggest the hushed whispers of witness as well. Lines such as " Some of the ears on the floor caught this scrap of his voice. Some of the ears on the floor were pressed to the ground" have an evocative parallel structure and create a haunting final image.

Suggestions for Writing

1. Take a familiar passage of prose that you find rhythmical, and break it into lines. Pay attention to the rhythm of the prose and to your reasons for breaking each line. Use such elements as caesura (or pauses) in a line to help create the rhythm. In a workshop, group members might each do the same passage of prose and then discuss the similarities and differences that result.

2. Consider the reasons Carolyn Forché chose to write "The Colonel" as a prose poem. What effect is created by the way she states so bluntly, "There is no other way to say this." Focus on a traumatic memory, one you have wanted to write about, perhaps, but couldn't quite find the way to tell the story. Emulate the "reportage," the directness of Forché's style in your lines.

PART THREE

A Collection of Readings

Sherman Alexie (B. 1966)

Indian Education

Crazy Horse came back to life
in a storage room of the Smithsonian,
his body rising from a wooden crate
mistakenly marked ANONYMOUS HOPI MALE.

Crazy Horse wandered the halls, found   5
the surface of the moon, Judy Garland
and her red shoes, a stuffed horse named
Comanche, the only surviving

member of the Seventh Cavalry
at Little Big Horn. Crazy Horse was found   10
in the morning by a security guard
who took him home and left him alone

in a room with cable television. Crazy Horse
watched a basketball game, every black and white
western, a documentary about a scientist   15
who travelled the Great Plains in the 1800s

measuring Indians and settlers, discovering
that the Indians were two inches taller
on average, and in some areas, the difference
in height exceeded a foot, which proved nothing   20

although Crazy Horse measured himself
against the fact of a mirror, traded faces
with a taxi driver and memorized the city,
folding, unfolding, his mapped heart.

1996

Sherman Alexie and Diane Thiel
(B. 1966 AND B. 1967)

A Conversation with Sherman Alexie

DIANE THIEL: Can you say a bit about working in different genres in your writing, and often crossing genres in a single book? A signature element in your books seems to be a fusion of forms. One wonders while reading: "Is this a poem or short story?" What distinctions do you see between genres? Do you think some distinctions are rather artificial? Has your relationship with the different forms changed at all in the evolution of your work?

SHERMAN ALEXIE: I suppose, as an Indian living in the United States, I'm used to crossing real and imaginary boundaries, and have, in fact, enjoyed a richer and crazier and more magical life precisely because I have fearlessly and fearfully crossed all sorts of those barriers. I guess I approach my poetry the same way I have approached every other thing in my life. I just don't like being told what to do. I write whatever feels and sounds right to me. At the beginning of my career, I wrote free verse with some formal influences, but I have lately been writing more formal verse with free verse influences. I don't feel the need to spend all my time living on either the free verse or the formal reservation. I want it all; hunger is my crime.

DT: And what about the fusion of poetry and story in your work, in *The Business of Fancydancing: Stories and Poems*, and in *One Stick Song* in particular. Could you tell me a bit more about crossing those barriers? Not many writers defy the genres, and I'm curious about your decision to collect the stories and poems together as you have. And also about your path towards the novels and screenplays. Did you feel you needed a larger or different kind of canvas to tell certain stories?

SA: The original decision to include poems and stories in the first collection, *The Business of Fancydancing*, was made by the Hanging Loose Press editors. I was only twenty-three years old when that book was accepted for publication, and didn't really know how to put a book together (I still don't know how!), so it was really an editorial decision. I guess those Hanging Loose guys understood my work was a blend of poetry and fiction, and since I was such a baby writer then, I think that fusion is just natural, maybe even reflexive. I have to work hard now to make a poem completely identifiable as a poem, and not as a hybrid. Of course, I still love hybrids. I'm a hybrid. So I think it was the Hanging Loose editors who helped me define myself as a poet. They're still my poetry publishers, and I'm very curious what they'll do with my next book, which will be mostly formal poems. I think my path toward novels and screenplays was, number one, the simple effort to make more money so I could be a full-time writer. But heck, I haven't published a novel in seven years, so I'm not sure I can be described as a novelist. I think I'm a poet with short story inclinations. And since screenplays and movies are poetic in structure and intent, I find that I'm much more comfortable writing screenplays than I am writing novels. I am currently working on my first nonfiction, a big book about four generations of Indian men in my family, and our relationship with war, and I've broken it down into fiction, nonfiction project, and poetry, so I'm really looking for a hybrid work here. In some sense, I feel this new book is a summation of all my themes until now. After this book, I think I'll be looking in some radical new directions.

DT: Could you speak a bit about converting literature for the screen? What are the different demands of the work in print and the work on the screen? What is your process? What useful advice have you received along the way? Was there any "advice" that you instinctively did not agree with?

SA: Although I have written two produced movies, and worked on screenplays for a half-dozen unproduced flicks, I still haven't figured out what works or what doesn't. I don't think the audiences for movies are nearly as forgiving or ambitious as the audiences for poetry or fiction. Ninety-nine percent of all movies ever made, from the most independent to the most capitalistic, from the crappy ones to the classics, are identical in structure. If poets worked like film-makers, we'd all be writing sonnets, only sonnets, and nothing else! Just try to make a movie out of "The Wasteland" or *Portrait of the Artist as a Young Man*. I want to make movies that are much more like poems, so I'll be making them myself for extremely low budgets. The best advice I've ever received: "Sherman, quit wasting your time in Hollywood!" Of course, I have completely ignored that advice.

DT: In *First Indian on the Moon,* the poem "The Alcoholic Love Poems" ends with the lines "All I said was 'When I used to drink, you're exactly the kind of Indian I loved to get drunk with.' Oh all my life in the past tense." How does the recognition of "past tense" in this poem affect your writing? Do you often feel as if you are writing about past selves, past injuries? Can you discuss how past meets present in your work?

SA: In my dictionary, "Indian" and "nostalgic" are synonyms. As colonized people, I think we're always looking to the past for some real and imaginary sense of purity and authenticity. But I hate my nostalgia. I think I'm pop-culture obsessed because I hope it's an antidote for the disease of nostalgia. So I think the past and present are always duking it out in my work. The Lone Ranger and Tonto will always be fistfighting.

DT: The title poem of your first book, *The Business of Fancydancing,* is a sestina, and I notice that an interest in using the various forms of poetry has persisted in your body of work. Who were your early influences of "formal" poetry? Why did you feel drawn to it? What do you think are some of the possibilities using form provides?

SA: Although I would certainly be defined as a free verse poet, I have always worked in traditional and invented forms. Though I've never recognized it before, the fact that the title poem of my first book is a sestina says a lot about my varied ambitions. My earliest interest in formalism came from individual poems, rather than certain poets. Marvell's "To His Coy Mistress," Roethke's "My Papa's Waltz," Gwendolyn Brooks's "We Real Cool," and Langston Hughes's "A Dream Deferred" are poems that come to mind as early formal poems I admired. Speaking both seriously and facetiously, I think I've spent my whole career rewriting "My Papa's Waltz" with an Indian twist. Lately, as I've been writing much more formally, with end rhyme, a tenuous dance with meter, and explicit form, I've discovered that in writing toward that end rhyme, that accented or unaccented syllable, or that stanza break, I am constantly surprising myself with new ideas, new vocabulary, and new ways of looking at the world. The conscious use of forms seems to have freed my subconscious.

DT: That's exactly how I feel about using form—that it has the power to free the subconscious. I've actually thought about Roethke's poem when reading your work. For me, too, it was one of the poems that startled me into poetry early on. It's an interesting poem to teach because of the range of reaction to it. Some—those who focus on the waltz and the horseplay—feel the tone to be much lighter. Others—those who concentrate more on the whisky on his breath, the way the child "hung on like death," and the ear scraping a buckle—feel that it's much darker. I think that the tug of the two different tones creates the true charge in the poem.

SA: I think the poem is incredibly sad and violent, and its sadness and violence is underscored by its gentle rhymes and rhythms. It's Mother Goose on acid maybe. I think that gentle music is a form of denial about the terror contained in the poem, or maybe it's the way kids think, huh? My dad wasn't violent, but he would leave us to go drinking, and would sometimes be gone for a few weeks. He was completely undependable and unpredictable. My wife's father was a scary and unpredictable alcoholic, charming and funny one moment, violent and caustic the next. So Roethke's poem, I think, is all about the unpredictability of the alcoholic father.

DT: I find the way the personal fuses with the political a very evocative element in your work. The love poem, for instance, is often simultaneously a political poem. Sometimes this is suggestive, but other times it is quite direct, even in the very title—as in "Seven Love Songs Which Include the Collected History of the United States of America." Could you discuss this fusion and how it evolved in your work.

SA: I've stated in other places that Indians are politicized from birth. I was five or six years old, standing in line to get free government food on the reservation, when I had my first political thought: "Hey, I'm in this line because I'm an Indian!" Of course, I was having a great time in that line with my very funny and highly verbose siblings and parents. I would guess my family, pound for pound, is one of the funniest in the world! So I was taught to fuse the political and the artistic, the poem and the punchline. It seems to me it is just as much nature as nurture. In terms of love, I was involved in a long-term love affair with a white woman, and our races and our political positions were always a subject of discussion and dissent. I am never, not even in my most intimate moments, completely free of my tribe.

DT: The poet Michael S. Harper (with whom I studied years ago) has a book entitled *History Is Your Own Heartbeat*. I've always been particularly interested in exploring history in a poem, but doing so via a very personal current. Was it a conscious choice for you—to take on all that history in your work, or did it just slowly become your subject matter? What writers influenced you, in the way the personal and the historical mesh?

SA: Generally speaking, I think Indians have a much longer memory than white Americans. Or perhaps we Indians hold more passionate grudges! But I think my work has been more autobiographical than historical. So maybe I've been a personal historian. A poet-memoirist. In the link between personal and world history, I think other Native American poets have influenced me most—Simon Ortiz, Adrian C. Louis, Joy Harjo, Leslie Silko, just to name a few, who are constantly aware of history. In Ortiz's book-length poem *From Sand Creek*, he weaves his personal history with the history of genocide in the United States, and creates a stunning brand of confessional poetry. Simon seems to be confessing in a royal voice, with a tribal "we" and not a narcissistic "I." I hope that's what I'm doing with my poems.

DT: I've been thinking as we talk that perhaps the reason you're drawn to form in poetry might have something to do with your attraction to repetition and refrains. Many of your poems employ a kind of elliptical repetition—in your chapbook *Water Flowing Home*, for instance, the poem "This Woman Speaks" has this kind of elliptical nature:

> This woman speaks, this
> woman, who loves me, speaks
> to another woman, her
> mother, this daughter
> speaks to her mother

Could you comment on your use of repetition and the cultural aspects of this?

SA: In my tribe, and in the Native American world, in general, repetition is sacred. All of our songs go on for hours: "This Indian will be coming around the mountain when he comes, when he comes, when he comes . . . " So I think repetition appeals to me on that tribal level, and it also appeals to me on a simple musical level. I want my poems to sound like tribal songs, and with repetition, I can sometimes make English sound like Salish. I also think that in terms of spirituality and prayer, repetition can sound a note of desperation. Think of Hopkins, "Pitched past pain." God can feel so far away. So we sinful slobs have to keep screaming until God pays attention.

DT: When I heard you read in New Mexico, I was struck by the performative aspect. I know you've been involved in a number of poetry slams and have held the title of Heavyweight Poetry Champion (or something like that). Do you think of a poem as something meant to be performed, and what are the different ways you've developed to make a poem come alive in the air?

SA: Story-tellers were telling stories long before they had the means to record them or write them down, so I think performance is primal. I know it feels primal to me. When I'm really doing well onstage, I feel almost as crazy and wonderful as I do when I'm writing the stuff. As a story-teller, I also feel a responsibility to my audience. I want them to feel as strongly about the work as I do. I want them to know how much I both love and hate it. If a poem is funny, I want to hear the laughter. If it's sad, I want to hear the tears.

DT: How did your "stand-up" readings develop? Was it something you always did, or did it develop as a kind of backlash to the often dry, humorless readings that can be a part of the literary world? Would you consider yourself an extrovert? Or do you just don that persona when you are performing?

SA: Most of the readings I've been to are so damn boring! We've got a lot of competition out there in the world. I have to be at least as good as Eminem or I'm dead! In my personal life, I'm an introvert. I spend most of my time alone, with my thoughts for company, and much prefer a book and a bathtub to any gathering of messy human beings. As a public performer, I "act." It's a strange thing. I become a slightly larger and more exaggerated version of myself.

DT: I hear a great deal of humor in your fiction and drama (and in your performances), but it's often more subtle in your poetry. How do you feel about humor in poetry, in general?

SA: I think my poems are very funny, but readers are not trained to laugh at poems. And I think funny poems are seriously devalued in the poetry world. I'd love to edit an anthology of humorous poems that are serious and great by any standard. I'd call it "Funny Poems." I think Auden is hilarious. I think Lucille Clifton is very funny. And Frost is to my mind an incredibly bitter Bob Newhart.

DT: There are many references to the dream world in your work, even when it's not explicitly a dream being explored. "Dead Letter Office," for instance, begins with a very believable occurrence— receiving a letter written in your native tongue that needs translating—but as the poem goes on, the experience feels increasingly surreal, and you traipse after the translator, "Big Mom," for years, "holding some brief letter from the past." I chose that poem as an example because it's not directly about a dream, and yet it feels decidedly like one.

SA: I was hydrocephalic at birth, had serious brain surgery at six months of age, and had epileptic seizures and was on serious sedatives until age seven, so I certainly have a more scarred and ragged brain than most. I don't know how to speak of it medically, but I'm sure my brain damage gives me all sorts of visions! I've always been nightmare-prone and insomniac, so sleep and the lack of sleep, and dreams and nightmares have always been my primary obsession. I was taking phenobarbital before I went to Kindergarten, so I was probably destined to be a poet, enit?

2004

John Ashbery (B. 1927)

Paradoxes and Oxymorons

The poem is concerned with language on a very plain level.
Look at it talking to you. You look out a window
Or pretend to fidget. You have it but you don't have it.
You miss it, it misses you. You miss each other.

The poem is sad because it wants to be yours, and cannot.   5
What's a plain level? It is that and other things.
Bringing a system of them into play. Play?
Well, actually, yes, but I consider play to be

A deeper outside thing, a dreamed role-pattern,
As in the division of grace these long August days   10
Without proof. Open-ended. And before you know
It gets lost in the steam and chatter of typewriters.

It has been played once more. I think you exist only
To tease me into doing it, on your level, and then you aren't there
Or have adopted a different attitude. And the poem   15
Has set me softly down beside you. The poem is you.

1981

W. H. Auden (1907–1973)

Musée des Beaux Arts

About suffering they were never wrong,
The Old Masters: how well they understood
Its human position; how it takes place
While someone else is eating or opening a window or just walking
    dully along;

How, when the aged are reverently, passionately waiting   5
For the miraculous birth, there always must be
Children who did not specially want it to happen, skating
On a pond at the edge of the wood:
They never forgot
That even the dreadful martyrdom must run its course   10
Anyhow in a corner, some untidy spot
Where the dogs go on with their doggy life and the torturer's horse
Scratches its innocent behind on a tree.

In Brueghel's *Icarus*, for instance: how everything turns away
Quite leisurely from the disaster; the ploughman may   15
Have heard the splash, the forsaken cry,
But for him it was not an important failure; the sun shone
As it had to on the white legs disappearing into the green
Water; and the expensive delicate ship that must have seen
Something amazing, a boy falling out of the sky,   20
Had somewhere to get to and sailed calmly on.

1940

Elizabeth Bishop (1911–1979)

One Art

The art of losing isn't hard to master;
so many things seem filled with the intent
to be lost that their loss is no disaster.

Lose something every day. Accept the fluster
of lost door keys, the hour badly spent.   5
The art of losing isn't hard to master.

Then practice losing farther, losing faster:
places, and names, and where it was you meant
to travel. None of these will bring disaster.

I lost my mother's watch. And look! my last, or   10
next-to-last, of three loved houses went.
The art of losing isn't hard to master.

I lost two cities, lovely ones. And, vaster,
some realms I owned, two rivers, a continent.
I miss them, but it wasn't a disaster.   15

—Even losing you (the joking voice, a gesture
I love) I shan't have lied. It's evident
the art of losing's not too hard to master
though it may look like (*Write* it!) like disaster.

1976

Robert Browning (1812–1889)

My Last Duchess

Ferrara

That's my last Duchess painted on the wall,
Looking as if she were alive. I call
That piece a wonder, now; Frà Pandolf's hands
Worked busily a day, and there she stands.
Will't please you sit and look at her? I said   5
"Frà Pandolf" by design, for never read
Strangers like you that pictured countenance,
The depth and passion of its earnest glance,
But to myself they turned (since none puts by
The curtain I have drawn for you, but I)   10
And seemed as they would ask me, if they durst,
How such a glance came there; so, not the first
Are you to turn and ask thus. Sir, 'twas not
Her husband's presence only, called that spot
Of joy into the Duchess' cheek: perhaps   15
Frà Pandolf chanced to say, "Her mantle laps
Over my lady's wrist too much," or "Paint
Must never hope to reproduce the faint
Half-flush that dies along her throat." Such stuff
Was courtesy, she thought, and cause enough   20
For calling up that spot of joy. She had
A heart—how shall I say?—too soon made glad,
Too easily impressed; she liked whate'er
She looked on, and her looks went everywhere.
Sir, 'twas all one! My favor at her breast,   25
The dropping of the daylight in the West,
The bough of cherries some officious fool
Broke in the orchard for her, the white mule
She rode with round the terrace—all and each
Would draw from her alike the approving speech,   30
Or blush, at least. She thanked men,—good! but thanked
Somehow—I know not how—as if she ranked
My gift of a nine-hundred-years-old name
With anybody's gift. Who'd stoop to blame
This sort of trifling? Even had you skill   35
In speech—which I have not—to make your will
Quite clear to such an one, and say "Just this

Or that in you disgusts me; here you miss,
Or there exceed the mark"—and if she let
Herself be lessoned so, nor plainly set   40
Her wits to yours, forsooth, and made excuse—
E'en then would be some stooping; and I choose
Never to stoop. Oh, sir, she smiled, no doubt,
Whene'er I passed her; but who passed without
Much the same smile? This grew; I gave commands;   45
Then all smiles stopped together. There she stands
As if alive. Will't please you rise? We'll meet
The company below, then. I repeat,
The Count your master's known munificence
Is ample warrant that no just pretense   50
Of mine for dowry will be disallowed;
Though his fair daughter's self, as I avowed
At starting, is my object. Nay, we'll go
Together down, sir. Notice Neptune, though,
Taming a sea-horse, thought a rarity,   55
Which Claus of Innsbruck cast in bronze for me!

1842

My Last Duchess. Ferrara, a city in northern Italy, is the scene. Browning may
have modeled his speaker after Alonzo, Duke of Ferrara (1533–1598). 3 *Frà
Pandolf* and 56 *Claus of Innsbruck*: fictitious names of artists.

Gerry Cambridge (B. 1959)

Goldfinch in Spring

That finch which sings above my head,
Last year's speckled egg, is now
A partner in some nest instead,
That finch which sings above my head,
Buff-gold dandy masked with red,
And hen on eggs upon some swaying bough
That finch which sings.   Above my head
Last year's speckled egg is now.

1995

Lewis Carroll
(Charles Lutwidge Dodgson)
(1832–1898)

Jabberwocky

'Twas brillig, and the slithy toves
    Did gyre and gimble in the wabe:
All mimsy were the borogoves,
    And the mome raths outgrabe.

"Beware the Jabberwock, my son!   5
    The jaws that bite, the claws that catch!
Beware the Jubjub bird, and shun
    The frumious Bandersnatch!"

He took his vorpal sword in hand;
    Long time the manxome foe he sought—   10
So rested he by the Tumtum tree
    And stood awhile in thought.

And, as in uffish thought he stood,
    The Jabberwock, with eyes of flame,
Came whiffling through the tulgey wood,   15
    And burbled as it came!

One, two! One, two! And through and through
    The vorpal blade went snicker-snack!
He left it dead, and with its head
    He went galumphing back.   20

"And hast thou slain the Jabberwock?
    Come to my arms, my beamish boy!
O frabjous day! Callooh, Callay!"
    He chortled in his joy.

'Twas brillig, and the slithy toves   25
    Did gyre and gimble in the wabe:
All mimsy were the borogoves,
    And the mome raths outgrabe.

1871

Jabberwocky. Fussy about pronunciation, Carroll in his preface to *The Hunting of the Snark* declares: "The first 'o' in 'borogoves' is pronounced like the 'o' in 'borrow.' I have heard people try to give it the sound of the 'o' in 'worry.' Such is Human Perversity." *Toves*, he adds, rimes with *groves*.

Judith Ortiz Cofer (B. 1952)

Quinceañera

My dolls have been put away like dead
children in a chest I will carry
with me when I marry.
I reach under my skirt to feel
a satin slip bought for this day. It is soft   5
as the inside of my thighs. My hair
has been nailed back with my mother's
black hairpins to my skull. Her hands
stretched my eyes open as she twisted
braids into a tight circle at the nape   10
of my neck. I am to wash my own clothes
and sheets from this day on, as if
the fluids of my body were poison, as if
the little trickle of blood I believe
travels from my heart to the world were   15
shameful. Is not the blood of saints and
men in battle beautiful? Do Christ's hands
not bleed into your eyes from His cross?
At night I hear myself growing and wake
to find my hands drifting of their own will   20
to soothe skin stretched tight
over my bones.
I am wound like the guts of a clock,
waiting for each hour to release me.

1987

Quinceañera. *Quinceañera*: a fifteen-year-old girl's coming-out party in Latin
cultures.

Wendy Cope (B. 1945)

Lonely Hearts

Can someone make my simple wish come true?
Male biker seeks female for touring fun.
Do you live in North London? Is it you?

Gay vegetarian whose friends are few,
I'm into music, Shakespeare and the sun.   5
Can someone make my simple wish come true?

Executive in search of something new—
Perhaps bisexual woman, arty, young.
Do you live in North London? Is it you?

Successful, straight and solvent? I am too—   10
Attractive Jewish lady with a son.
Can someone make my simple wish come true?

I'm Libran, inexperienced and blue—
Need slim non-smoker, under twenty-one.
Do you live in North London? Is it you?   15

Please write (with photo) to Box 152.
Who knows where it may lead once we've begun?
Can someone make my simple wish come true?
Do you live in North London? Is it you?

1986

Hart Crane (1899–1932)

My Grandmother's Love Letters

There are no stars tonight
But those of memory.
Yet how much room for memory there is
In the loose girdle of soft rain.

There is even room enough   5
For the letters of my mother's mother,
Elizabeth,
That have been pressed so long
Into a corner of the roof
That they are brown and soft,   10
And liable to melt as snow.

Over the greatness of such space
Steps must be gentle.
It is all hung by an invisible white hair.
It trembles as birch limbs webbing the air.   15

And I ask myself:

"Are your fingers long enough to play
Old keys that are but echoes:
Is the silence strong enough
To carry back the music to its source   20
And back to you again
As though to her?"

Yet I would lead my grandmother by the hand
Through much of what she would not understand;
And so I stumble. And the rain continues on the roof   25
With such a sound of gently pitying laughter.

1926

Paul Laurence Dunbar (1872–1906)

We Wear the Mask

We wear the mask that grins and lies,
It hides our cheeks and shades our eyes—
This debt we pay to human guile;
With torn and bleeding hearts we smile,
And mouth with myriad subtleties. 5

Why should the world be over-wise,
In counting all our tears and sighs?
Nay, let them only see us, while
 We wear the mask.

We smile, but O great Christ, our cries 10
To thee from tortured souls arise.
We sing, but oh the clay is vile
Beneath our feel, and long the mile;
But let the world dream otherwise,
We wear the mask! 15

1896

Rhina P. Espaillat (B. 1932)

Bilingual/Bilingüe

My father liked them separate, one there,
one here (allá y aquí), as if aware

that words might cut in two his daughter's heart
(el corazón) and lock the alien part

to what he was—his memory, his name   5
(su nombre)—with a key he could not claim.

"English outside this door, Spanish inside,"
he said, "y basta." But who can divide

the world, the word (mundo y palabra) from
any child? I knew how to be dumb   10

and stubborn (testaruda); late, in bed,
I hoarded secret syllables I read

until my tongue (mi lengua) learned to run
where his stumbled. And still the heart was one.

I like to think he knew that, even when,   15
proud (orgulloso) of his daughter's pen,

he stood outside mis versos, half in fear
of words he loved but wanted not to hear.

1998

Bilingual/Bilingüe

Recent interest in the phenomenon known as "Spanglish" has led me to reexamine my own experience as a writer who works chiefly in her second language, and especially to recall my father's inflexible rule against the mixing of languages. In fact, no English was allowed in that midtown Manhattan apartment that became home after my arrival in New York in 1939. My father read the daily paper in English, taught himself to follow disturbing events in Europe through the medium of English-language radio, and even taught me to read the daily comic strips, in an effort to speed my learning of the language he knew I would need. But that necessary language was banished from family conversation: it was the medium of the outer world, beyond the door; inside, among ourselves, only Spanish was permitted, and it had to be pure, grammatical, unadulterated Spanish.

At the age of seven, however, nothing seems more important than communicating with classmates and neighborhood children. For my mother, too, the new language was a way out of isolation, a means to deal with the larger world and with those American women for whom she sewed. But my father, a political exile waiting for changes in our native country, had different priorities: he lived in the hope of return, and believed that the new home, the new speech, were temporary. His theory was simple: if it could be said at all, it could be said best in the language of those authors whose words were the core of his education. But his insistence on pure Spanish made it difficult, sometimes impossible, to bring home and share the jokes of friends, puns, pop lyrics, and other staples of seven-year-old conversation. Table talk sometimes ended with tears or sullen silence.

And yet, despite the friction it caused from time to time, my native language was also a source of comfort—the reading that I loved, intimacy within the family, and a peculiar auditory delight best described as echoes in the mind. I learned early to relish words as counters in a game that could turn suddenly serious without losing the quality of play, and to value their sound as a meaning behind their meaning.

Nostalgia, a confusion of identity, the fear that if the native language is lost the self will somehow be altered forever: all are part of the subtle flavor of immigrant life, as well as the awareness that one owes gratitude to strangers for acts of communication that used to be simple and once imposed no such debt.

Memory, folklore, and food all become part of the receding landscape that language sets out to preserve. Guilt, too, adds to the mix, the suspicion that to love the second language too much is to betray those ancestors who spoke the first and could not communicate with us in the vocabulary of our education, our new thoughts. And finally, a sense of grievance and loss may spur hostility toward the new language and those who speak it, as if the common speech of the perceived majority could weld together a disparate population into a huge, monolithic, and threatening Other. That Other is then assigned traits and habits that preclude sympathy and mold "Us" into a unity whose cohesiveness gives comfort.

Luckily, there is another side to bilingualism: curiosity about the Other may be as natural and pervasive as group loyalty. If it weren't, travel, foreign residence, and intermarriage would be less common than they are. For some bilingual writers, the Other—and the language he speaks—are appealing. Some acknowledge and celebrate the tendency of languages to borrow from each other and produce something different in the process. That is, in part, the tendency that has given rise to "Spanglish."

It's dangerous, however, to accept the inevitable melding of languages over time as a justification for speaking, in the short run, a mix that impoverishes both languages by allowing words in one to drive out perfectly good equivalent words in the other. The habitual speaker of such a mix ends by speaking not two, or even one complete language, but fragments of two that are no longer capable of standing alone or serving the speaker well with any larger audience. As a literary device with limited appeal and durability, "Spanglish," like other such blends, is expressive and fresh. But as a substitute for genuine biliguality—the cultivation and preservation of two languages—I suspect it represents a danger to the advancement of foreign speakers, and a loss to both cultures. My father sensed as much in 1939, and stubbornly preserved my native language for me, through his insistence that I be truly bilingual rather than a traveler across boundaries that "Spanglish" has made all too permeable.

My father, who never learned to think in English, was persuaded that the words of his own language were the "true" names for things in the world. But for me that link between fact and word was broken, as it is for many who grow up bilingual. Having been taught to love words and take them seriously as reflections of reality, I felt it a loss to learn that, in fact, words are arbitrary, man-made, no more permanent than clothing: somewhere under all of them reality is naked.

Disconcerting as it is, however, to lose the security of words that are perceived as single keys to what they unlock, it is also exhilarating to see oneself as the maker of those words, even if they are now impermanent, provisional artifacts that have value for us only because they're ours. Anybody who has ever gone hunting for that one right and elusive word knows what bilingualism feels like, even if he's never left his native country or learned a word in any language but his own. There is a sense in which every poet is bilingual, and those of us who are more overtly so are only living metaphors for the condition that applies to us all. We use a language that seems deceptively like the language of the people around us, but isn't quite. The words are the same, but the weight we give them, the connections we find among them, the criteria we use to choose this one rather than that one, are our own.

At a recent poetry reading I closed with a poem in Spanish, and a member of the English-speaking audience approached me afterward to remark how moved she had been by that poem, and how she wished I had read others.

"Where did you learn Spanish?" I asked.

"I don't speak any Spanish," she replied. "What I understood was the music of what you read."

It occurred to me, during our subsequent conversation, that poetry may be precisely what is almost lost, not in translation, but in the wording, the transit from experience to paper. If we succeed in salvaging anything, maybe it is most often in the music, the formal elements of poetry that do travel from language to language, as the formal music of classic Spanish poetry my father loved followed me into English and draws me, to this day, to poems that are patterned and rich and playful.

It's occurred to me since that conversation that a poem in Spanish may have more in common with a poem in English—or any other language—than with a grocery list, say, or a piece of technical writing that happens to use Spanish words. There is something in poetry that transcends specific language, that makes it possible for transplanted people like me to recognize the songs of the Other as his own even before he understands them fully. Poetry may be used to draw very small circles around itself, identifying its speaker as a member of a narrowly delineated group and looking at "outsiders" with eyes that discern less and less detail as distance increases. But it may also be used to draw very large circles, circles that will draw in rather than exclude, as in Edwin Markham's apt four-line metaphor titled "Outwitted":

He drew a circle that shut me out—
Heretic, rebel, a thing to flout.
But Love and I had the wit to win:
We drew a circle that shut him in.

1998

Lawrence Ferlinghetti (B. 1919)

Don't Let That Horse
Eat That Violin

Don't let that horse
          eat that violin

    cried Chagall's mother
          But he
       kept right on   5
          painting
And became famous
And kept on painting
          The Horse With Violin In Mouth
And when he finally finished it   10
he jumped up upon the horse
          and rode away
      waving the violin
And then with a low bow gave it
to the first naked nude he ran across   15
And there were no strings
          attached

                        1955

Carolyn Forché (B. 1950)

The Colonel

What you have heard is true. I was in his house. His wife carried a tray of coffee and sugar. His daughter filed her nails, his son went out for the night. There were daily papers, pet dogs, a pistol on the cushion beside him. The moon swung bare on its black cord over the house. On the television was a cop show. It was in English. Broken bottles were embedded in the walls around the house to scoop the kneecaps from a man's legs or cut his hands to lace. On the windows there were gratings like those in liquor stores. We had dinner, rack of lamb, good wine, a gold bell was on the table for calling the maid. The maid brought green mangoes, salt, a type of bread. I was asked how I enjoyed the country. There was a brief commercial in Spanish. His wife took everything away. There was some talk then of how difficult it had become to govern. The parrot said hello on the terrace. The colonel told it to shut up, and pushed himself from the table. My friend said to me with his eyes: say nothing. The colonel returned with a sack used to bring groceries home. He spilled many human ears on the table. They were like dried peach halves. There is no other way to say this. He took one of them in his hands, shook it in our faces, dropped it into a water glass. It came alive there. I am tired of fooling around he said. As for the rights of anyone, tell your people they can go fuck themselves. He swept the ears to the floor with his arm and held the last of his wine in the air. Something for your poetry, no? he said. Some of the ears on the floor caught this scrap of his voice. Some of the ears on the floor were pressed to the ground.

MAY 1978

1981

Robert Frost (1874–1963)

The Road Not Taken

Two roads diverged in a yellow wood,
And sorry I could not travel both
And be one traveler, long I stood
And looked down one as far as I could
To where it bent in the undergrowth;   5

Then took the other, as just as fair,
And having perhaps the better claim,
Because it was grassy and wanted wear;
Though as for that the passing there
Had worn them really about the same,   10

And both that morning equally lay
In leaves no step had trodden black.
Oh, I kept the first for another day!
Yet knowing how way leads on to way,
I doubted if I should ever come back.   15

I shall be telling this with a sigh
Somewhere ages and ages hence:
Two roads diverged in a wood, and I—
I took the one less traveled by,
And that has made all the difference.   20

1916

"Out, Out—"

The buzz-saw snarled and rattled in the yard
And made dust and dropped stove-length sticks of wood,
Sweet-scented stuff when the breeze drew across it.
And from there those that lifted eyes could count
Five mountain ranges one behind the other   5
Under the sunset far into Vermont.
And the saw snarled and rattled, snarled and rattled,
As it ran light, or had to bear a load.
And nothing happened: day was all but done.
Call it a day, I wish they might have said   10
To please the boy by giving him the half hour
That a boy counts so much when saved from work.
His sister stood beside them in her apron
To tell them "Supper." At the word, the saw,
As if to prove saws knew what supper meant,   15
Leaped out at the boy's hand, or seemed to leap—
He must have given the hand. However it was,
Neither refused the meeting. But the hand!
The boy's first outcry was a rueful laugh,
As he swung toward them holding up the hand   20
Half in appeal, but half as if to keep
The life from spilling. Then the boy saw all—
Since he was old enough to know, big boy
Doing a man's work, though a child at heart—
He saw all spoiled. "Don't let him cut my hand off—   25
The doctor, when he comes. Don't let him, sister!"
So. But the hand was gone already.
The doctor put him in the dark of ether.
He lay and puffed his lips out with his breath.
And then—the watcher at his pulse took fright.   30
No one believed. They listened at his heart.
Little—less—nothing!—and that ended it.
No more to build on there. And they, since they
Were not the one dead, turned to their affairs.

1916

Poetic Metaphor (from "Education by Poetry")

I do not think anybody ever knows the discreet use of metaphors, his own and other people's, the discreet handling of metaphor, unless he has been properly educated in poetry.

Poetry begins in trivial metaphors, pretty metaphors, "grace" metaphors, and goes on to the profoundest thinking that we have. Poetry provides the one permissible way of saying one thing and meaning another. People say, "why don't you say what you mean?" We never do that, do we, being all of us too much poets. We like to talk in parables and in hints and in indirections—whether from diffidence or some other instinct.

I have wanted in late years to go further and further in making metaphor the whole of thinking. I find someone now and then to agree with me that all thinking, except mathematical thinking, is metaphorical, or all thinking except scientific thinking. The mathematical might be difficult for me to bring in, but the scientific is easy enough.

What I am pointing out is that unless you are at home in the metaphor, unless you have had your proper poetical education in the metaphor, you are not safe anywhere. Because you are not at ease with figurative values: you don't know the metaphor in its strength and its weakness. You don't know how far you may expect to ride it and when it may break down with you. You are not safe in science; you are not safe in history.

1930

Dana Gioia (B. 1950)

My Confessional Sestina

Let me confess. I'm sick of these sestinas
written by youngsters in poetry workshops
for the delectation of their fellow students,
and then published in little magazines
that no one reads, not even the contributors   5
who at least in this omission show some taste.

Is this merely a matter of personal taste?
I don't think so. Most sestinas
are such dull affairs. Just ask the contributors
the last time they finished one outside of a workshop,   10
even the poignant one on herpes in that new little magazine
edited by their most brilliant fellow student.

Let's be honest. It has become a form for students,
an exercise to build technique rather than taste
and the official entry blank into the little magazines—   15
because despite its reputation, a passable sestina
isn't very hard to write, even for kids in workshops
who care less about being poets than contributors.

Granted nowadays everyone is a contributor.
My barber is currently a student   20
in a rigorous correspondence school workshop.
At lesson six he can already taste
success having just placed his own sestina
in a national tonsorial magazine.

Who really cares about most little magazines?   25
Eventually not even their own contributors
who having published a few preliminary sestinas
send their work East to prove they're no longer students.
They need to be recognized as the new arbiters of taste
so they can teach their own graduate workshops.   30

Where will it end? This grim cycle of workshops
churning out poems for little magazines
no one honestly finds to their taste?
This ever-lengthening column of contributors

scavenging the land for more students   35
teaching them to write their boot-camp sestinas?

Perhaps there is an afterlife where all contributors
have two workshops, a tasteful little magazine, and sexy students
who worshipfully memorize their every sestina.

                                                        1991

R. S. Gwynn (B. 1948)

Shakespearean Sonnet

(With a first line taken from the tv listings)

A man is haunted by his father's ghost.
Boy meets girl while feuding families fight.
A Scottish king is murdered by his host.
Two couples get lost on a summer night.
A hunchback murders all who block his way.   5
A ruler's rivals plot against his life.
A fat man and a prince make rebels pay.
A noble Moor has doubts about his wife.
An English king decides to conquer France.
A duke learns that his best friend is a she.   10
A forest sets the scene for this romance.
An old man and his daughters disagree.
A Roman leader makes a big mistake.
A sexy queen is bitten by a snake.

2001

Donald Hall (B. 1928)

Names of Horses

All winter your brute shoulders strained against collars, padding
and steerhide over the ash hames, to haul
sledges of cordwood for drying through spring and summer,
for the Glenwood stove next winter, and for the simmering range.

In April you pulled cartloads of manure to spread on the fields,   5
dark manure of Holsteins, and knobs of your own clustered with
   oats.
All summer you mowed the grass in meadow and hayfield, the
   mowing machine
clacketing beside you, while the sun walked high in the morning;

and after noon's heat, you pulled a clawed rake through the same
   acres,
gathering stacks, and dragged the wagon from stack to stack,   10
and the built hayrack back, uphill to the chaffy barn,
three loads of hay a day from standing grass in the morning.   5

Sundays you trotted the two miles to church with the light load
of a leather quartertop buggy, and grazed in the sound of hymns.
Generation on generation, your neck rubbed the windowsill   15
of the stall, smoothing the wood as the sea smooths glass.

When you were old and lame, when your shoulders hurt bending to
   graze,
one October the man, who fed you and kept you, and harnessed you
   every morning,
led you through corn stubble to sandy ground above Eagle Pond,
and dug a hole beside you where you stood shuddering in your skin,   20

and lay the shotgun's muzzle in the boneless hollow behind your ear,   10
and fired the slug into your brain, and felled you into your grave,
shoveling sand to cover you, setting goldenrod upright above you,
where by next summer a dent in the ground made your monument.

For a hundred and fifty years, in the pasture of dead horses,   25
roots of pine trees pushed through the pale curves of your ribs,
yellow blossoms flourished above you in autumn, and in winter
frost heaved your bones in the ground—old toilers, soil makers:

O Roger, Mackerel, Riley, Ned, Nellie, Chester, Lady Ghost.

1978

Joy Harjo (B. 1951)

She Had Some Horses

She had some horses.
She had horses who were bodies of sand.
She had horses who were maps drawn of blood.
She had horses who were skins of ocean water.
She had horses who were the blue air of sky. 5
She had horses who were fur and teeth.
She had horses who were clay and would break.
She had horses who were splintered red cliff.

She had some horses.

She had horses with long, pointed breasts. 10
She had horses with full, brown thighs.
She had horses who laughed too much.
She had horses who threw rocks at glass houses.
She had horses who licked razor blades.

She had some horses. 15

She had horses who danced in their mothers' arms.
She had horses who thought they were the sun and their
bodies shone and burned like stars.
She had horses who waltzed nightly on the moon.
She had horses who were much too shy, and kept quiet 20
in stalls of their own making.

She had some horses.

She had horses who liked Creek Stomp Dance songs.
She had horses who cried in their beer.
She had horses who spit at male queens who made 25
them afraid of themselves.
She had horses who said they weren't afraid.
She had horses who lied.
She had horses who told the truth, who were stripped
bare of their tongues. 30

She had some horses.

She had horses who called themselves, "horse".
She had horses who called themselves, "spirit", and kept
their voices secret and to themselves.
She had horses who had no names. 35
She had horses who had books of names.

She had some horses.

She had horses who whispered in the dark, who were afraid to speak.
She had horses who screamed out of fear of the silence, who
carried knives to protect themselves from ghosts.   40
She had horses who waited for destruction.
She had horses who waited for resurrection.

She had some horses.

She had horses who got down on their knees for any saviour.
She had horses who thought their high price had saved them.   45
She had horses who tried to save her, who climbed in her
bed at night and prayed as they raped her.

She had some horses.

She had some horses she loved.
She had some horses she hated.   50

These were the same horses.

                                                        1983

Michael S. Harper (B. 1938)

Dear John,
Dear Coltrane

a love supreme, a love supreme
a love supreme, a love supreme

Sex fingers toes
in the marketplace
near your father's church
in Hamlet, North Carolina—
witness to this love   5
in this calm fallow
of these minds,
there is no substitute for pain:
genitals gone or going,
seed burned out,   10
you tuck the roots in the earth,
turn back, and move
by river through the swamps,
singing: *a love supreme, a love supreme;*
what does it all mean?   15
Loss, so great each black
woman expects your failure
in mute change, the seed gone.
You plod up into the electric city—
your song now crystal and   20
the blues. You pick up the horn
with some will and blow
into the freezing night:
a love supreme, a love supreme—

Dawn comes and you cook   25
up the thick sin 'tween
impotence and death, fuel
the tenor sax cannibal
heart, genitals, and sweat
that makes you clean—   30
a love supreme, a love supreme—
Why you so black?
cause I am
why you so funky?

cause I am　　　　　　　　　　　　　　　　　　　　35
why you so black?
cause I am
why you so sweet?
cause I am
why you so black?　　　　　　　　　　　　　　　40
cause I am
a love supreme, a love supreme:

So sick
you couldn't play *Naima*,
so flat we ached　　　　　　　　　　　　　　　　45
for song you'd concealed
with your own blood,
your diseased liver gave
out its purity,
the inflated heart　　　　　　　　　　　　　　　50
pumps out, the tenor kiss,
tenor love:
a love supreme, a love supreme—
a love supreme, a love supreme—

　　　　　　　　　　　　　　　　　　　1970

Langston Hughes (1902–1967)

The Weary Blues

Droning a drowsy syncopated tune,
Rocking back and forth to a mellow croon,
   I heard a Negro play.
Down on Lenox Avenue the other night
By the pale dull pallor of an old gas light   5
   He did a lazy sway. . . .
   He did a lazy sway. . . .
To the tune o' those Weary Blues.
With his ebony hands on each ivory key
He made that poor piano moan with melody.   10
   O Blues!
Swaying to and fro on his rickety stool
He played that sad raggy tune like a musical fool.
   Sweet Blues!
Coming from a black man's soul.   15
   O Blues!
In a deep song voice with a melancholy tone
I heard that Negro sing, that old piano moan—
   "Ain't got nobody in all this world,
     Ain't got nobody but ma self.   20
     I's gwine to quit ma frownin'
     And put ma troubles on the shelf."

Thump, thump, thump, went his foot on the floor.
He played a few chords then he sang some more—
   "I got the Weary Blues   25
     And I can't be satisfied.
     Got the Weary Blues
     And can't be satisfied—
     I ain't happy no mo'
     And I wish that I had died."   30
And far into the night he crooned that tune.
The stars went out and so did the moon.
The singer stopped playing and went to bed
While the Weary Blues echoed through his head.
He slept like a rock or a man that's dead.   35

1926

The Weary Blues. This poem quotes the first blues song Hughes had ever heard, "The Weary Blues," which begins, "I got de weary blues / And I can't be satisfied / . . . I ain't happy no mo'/ And I wish that I had died."

Nikos Kavadias (1913–1975)

A Knife

I always carry, tight on my belt,
a small African knife I've had for years—
the kind that are commonly seen in the North,
which I bought from an old merchant in Algiers.

I remember, as if it were now, the old dealer   5
who looked like a Goya oil painting,
standing next to long swords and torn
uniforms—in a hoarse voice, saying,

"This knife, here, which you want to buy—
legend surrounds it. Everyone knows   10
that those who have owned it, one after another
have all, at some time, killed someone close.

Don Basilio used it to kill
Donna Giulia, his unfaithful wife.
And Count Antonio, one night, secretly   15
murdered his brother with this knife.

Some Italian sailor—a Greek boatswain.
An African, in a jealous rage, his lover.
Hand to hand, it fell into mine.
I've seen many things, but this brings me terror.   20

Bend down. Look. Here, hold it. It's light.
And see here, the anchor and coat of arms.
But I would advise you to buy something else.
How much? Seven francs. Since you want it, it's yours."

This dagger now tight in my belt—my strangeness   25
made me take it off that shelf.
Since there's no one I hate enough to kill,
I fear someday I'll turn it on myself.

1936; trans. 2003

Translated by Diane Thiel

John Keats (1795–1821)

Ode on a Grecian Urn

Thou still unravished bride of quietness,
   Thou foster-child of silence and slow time,
Sylvan historian, who canst thus express
   A flowery tale more sweetly than our rhyme:
What leaf-fringed legend haunts about thy shape   5
   Of deities or mortals, or of both,
      In Tempe or the dales of Arcady?
   What men or gods are these? What maidens loth?
What mad pursuit? What struggle to escape?
      What pipes and timbrels? What wild ecstasy?   10

Heard melodies are sweet, but those unheard
   Are sweeter; therefore, ye soft pipes, play on;
Not to the sensual° ear, but, more endeared,   *physical*
   Pipe to the spirit ditties of no tone:
Fair youth, beneath the trees, thou canst not leave   15
   Thy song, nor ever can those trees be bare;
      Bold Lover, never, never canst thou kiss,
Though winning near the goal—yet, do not grieve;
      She cannot fade, though thou hast not thy bliss,
   For ever wilt thou love, and she be fair!   20

Ah, happy, happy boughs! that cannot shed
   Your leaves, nor ever bid the Spring adieu;
And, happy melodist, unwearièd,
   For ever piping songs for ever new;
More happy love! more happy, happy love!   25
   For ever warm and still to be enjoyed,
      For ever panting, and for ever young;
All breathing human passion far above,
   That leaves a heart high-sorrowful and cloyed,
      A burning forehead, and a parching tongue.   30

Who are these coming to the sacrifice?
   To what green altar, O mysterious priest,
Lead'st thou that heifer lowing at the skies,
   And all her silken flanks with garlands drest?
What little town by river or sea shore,   35
   Or mountain-built with peaceful citadel,
      Is emptied of this folk, this pious morn?
And, little town, the streets for evermore

Will silent be; and not a soul to tell
    Why thou art desolate, can e'er return.   40
O Attic shape! Fair attitude! with brede°   *design*
    Of marble men and maidens overwrought,
With forest branches and the trodden weed;
    Thou, silent form, dost tease us out of thought
As doth Eternity: Cold Pastoral!   45
    When old age shall this generation waste,
        Thou shalt remain, in midst of other woe
    Than ours, a friend to man, to whom thou say'st,
Beauty is truth, truth beauty,—that is all
    Ye know on earth, and all ye need to know.   50

                                 1820

Ode on a Grecian Urn. 7 *Tempe, dales of Arcady*: valleys in Greece. 41 *Attic*: Athenian, possessing a classical simplicity and grace. 49–50: if Keats had put the urn's words in quotation marks, critics might have been spared much ink. Does the urn say just "beauty is truth, truth beauty," or does its statement take in the whole of the last two lines?

Yusef Komunyakaa (B. 1947)

Rhythm Method

If you were sealed inside a box
within a box deep in a forest,
with no birdsongs, no crickets
rubbing legs together, no leaves
letting go of mottled branches,   5
you'd still hear the rhythm
of your heart. A red tide
of beached fish oscillates in sand,
copulating beneath a full moon,
& we can call this the first   10
rhythm because sex is what
nudged the tongue awake
& taught the hand to hit
drums & embrace reed flutes
before they were worked   15
from wood & myth. Up
& down, in & out, the piston
drives a dream home. Water
drips till it sculpts a cup
into a slab of stone.   20
At first, no bigger
than a thimble, it holds
joy, but grows to measure
the rhythm of loneliness
that melts sugar in tea.   25
There's a season for snakes
to shed rainbows on the grass,
for locust to chant out of the dunghill.
Oh yes, oh yes, oh yes, oh yes
is a confirmation the skin   30
sings to hands. The Mantra
of spring rain opens the rose
& spider lily into shadow,
& someone plays the bones
till they rise & live   35
again. We know the whole weight
depends on small silences
we fit ourselves into.
High heels at daybreak

is the saddest refrain. 40
If you can see blues
in the ocean, light & dark,
can feel worms ease through
a subterranean path
beneath each footstep, 45
Baby, you got rhythm.

1998

Shirley Geok-Lin Lim (B. 1944)

Pantoum for Chinese Women

*"At present, the phenomenon of butchering, drowning, and
leaving to die female infants has been very serious."*
—(PEOPLE'S DAILY OF BEIJING, MARCH 3, 1983)

They say a child with two mouths is no good.
In the slippery wet, a hollow space
Smooth gumming, echoing wide for food.
No wonder my man is not here at his place.

In the slippery wet, a hollow space, 5
a slit narrowly sheathed within its hood.
No wonder my man is not here at his place:
He is digging for the dragon jar of soot,

that slit, narrowly sheathed within its hood!
His mother, squatting, coughs by the fire's blaze 10
while he digs for the dragon jar of soot.
We had saved ashes for a hundred days.

His mother, squatting, coughs by the fire's blaze.
The child kicks against me, mewing like a flute.
We had saved ashes for a hundred days, 15
knowing, if the time came, that we would.

The child kicks against me, crying like a flute
Through its two weak mouths. His mother prays,
Knowing when the time comes, that we would,
For broken clay is never set in glaze. 20

Through her two weak mouths his mother prays.
She will not pluck the rooster, nor serve its blood,
For broken clay is never set in glaze:
Women are made of river sand and wood.

She will not pluck the rooster nor serve its blood. 25
My husband frowns, pretending in his haste
Women are made of river sand and wood.
Milk soaks the bedding. I cannot bear the waste.

My husband frowns, pretending in his haste.
Oh clean the girl, dress her in ashy soot!   30
Milk soaks our bedding. I cannot bear the waste.
They say a child with two mouths is no good.

1994

April Lindner (B. 1962)

Spice

I save jars for the transparent hope
of what they'll hold, and later I save
what's in those jars past pungency,

lug them from one city to the next.
My pantry's bottom shelf recalls   5
an Indian grocery, bolts of silvered cloth,

sitar on eight-track tapes. The homesick owner
fussed over his only Anglo customer,
guiding me through the dusty shelves out back

past lentils, yellow, pink, and black,   10
past burlap sacks of *basmati*, to the spices
whose names I loved, whose perfumes I had to own:

garam masala, amchoor, fenugreek,
even *asafetida,* the fetid root
whose musk seeps through mason glass   15

to fog the air with gold. Saffron filaments,
cardamom pods, black and green.
Here's a souvenir mailed from Barbados,

nutmegs ground to slivers, impossible
to grate without shredding finger skin,   20
and from an Asian market in Toledo

this powder I bought for its pretty bottle
and licked from my palm on the drive home—
orange peel? red pepper? poppy seed?—

conjuring cool tatami floors, rice paper,   25
a tea ceremony's slow unfolding. Now I linger
at this small glass skyline in the shadows,

this shrine to continents I planned to reach
and haven't yet, my fingertips burnished,
the air a billowing veil of coriander.   30

2002

David Mason (B. 1954)

Acrostic from Aegina

Anemones you brought back from the path
Nod in a glass beside our rumpled bed.
Now you are far away. In the aftermath
Even these flowers arouse my sleepy head.

Love, when I think of the ready look in your eyes,   5
Erotas that would make these stone walls blush
Nerves me to write away the morning's hush.
Nadir of longing, and the red anemones
Over the lucent rim—my poor designs,
X-rated praise I've hidden between these lines.   10

2004

Marianne Moore (1887–1972)

Poetry

I too, dislike it: there are things that are important beyond all this
                    fiddle.
    Reading it, however, with a perfect contempt for it, one discovers
                that there is in
  it after all, a place for the genuine.
      Hands that can grasp, eyes
        that can dilate, hair that can rise   5
            if it must, these things are important not because a
high sounding interpretation can be put upon them but because they
                    are
  useful; when they become so derivative as to become
                unintelligible, the
same thing may be said for all of us—that we
    do not admire what   10
    we cannot understand. The bat,
        holding on upside down or in quest of something to
eat, elephants pushing, a wild horse taking a roll, a tireless wolf under
a tree, the immovable critic twinkling his skin like a horse that
                feels a flea, the base-
ball fan, the statistician—case after case   15
    could be cited did
    one wish it; nor is it valid
      to discriminate against "business documents and
school-books"; all these phenomena are important. One must make a
                distinction
  however: when dragged into prominence by half poets, the result
                is not poetry,   20
  nor till the autocrats among us can be
    "literalists of
    the imagination"—above
      insolence and triviality and can present
for inspection, imaginary gardens with real toads in them, shall we
                have   25

it. In the meantime, if you demand on one hand, in defiance of
               their opinion—
the raw material of poetry in
    all its rawness and
    that which is, on the other hand,
        genuine then you are interested in poetry.   30

                                     1921

Frederick Morgan (B. 1922)

1904

The things they did together, no one knew
It was late June. Behind the old wood-shed
wild iris was in blossom, white and blue,
but what those proud ones did there, no one knew,
though some suspected there were one or two   5
who led the others where they would be led.
Years passed—but what they did there, no one knew,
those summer children long since safely dead.

1987

Marilyn Nelson (B. 1946)

Chosen

Diverne wanted to die, that August night
his face hung over hers, a sweating moon.
She wished so hard, she killed part of her heart.

If she had died, her one begotten son,
her life's one light, would never have been born.   5
Pomp Atwood might have been another man:

born with a single race, another name.
Diverne might not have known the starburst joy
her son would give her. And the man who came

out of a twelve-room house and ran to her   10
close shack across three yards that night, to leap
onto her cornshuck pallet. Pomp was their

share of the future. And it wasn't rape.
In spite of her raw terror. And his whip.

1990

Naomi Shihab Nye (B. 1952)

Famous

The river is famous to the fish.

The loud voice is famous to silence,
which knew it would inherit the earth
before anybody said so.

The cat sleeping on the fence is famous to the birds   5
watching him from the birdhouse.

The tear is famous, briefly, to the cheek.

The idea you carry close to your bosom
is famous to your bosom.

The boot is famous to the earth,   10
more famous than the dress shoe,
which is famous only to floors.

The bent photograph is famous to the one who carries it
and not at all famous to the one who is pictured.

I want to be famous to shuffling men   15
who smile while crossing streets,
sticky children in grocery lines,
famous as the one who smiled back.

I want to be famous in the way a pulley is famous,
or a buttonhole, not because it did anything spectacular,   20
but because it never forgot what it could do.

1982

Craig Raine (B. 1944)

A Martian Sends a Postcard Home

Caxtons are mechanical birds with many wings
and some are treasured for their markings—

they cause the eyes to melt
or the body to shriek without pain.

I have never seen one fly, but   5
sometimes they perch on the hand.

Mist is when the sky is tired of flight
and rests its soft machine on ground:

then the world is dim and bookish
like engravings under tissue paper.   10

Rain is when the earth is television.
It has the property of making colours darker.

Model T is a room with the lock inside—
a key is turned to free the world

for movement, so quick there is a film   15
to watch for anything missed.

But time is tied to the wrist
or kept in a box, ticking with impatience.

In homes, a haunted apparatus sleeps,
that snores when you pick it up.   20

If the ghost cries, they carry it
to their lips and soothe it to sleep

with sounds. And yet, they wake it up
deliberately, by tickling with a finger.

Only the young are allowed to suffer   25
openly. Adults go to a punishment room

with water but nothing to eat.
They lock the door and suffer the noises

alone. No one is exempt
and everyone's pain has a different smell.   30

At night, when all the colours die,
they hide in pairs

and read about themselves—
in colour, with their eyelids shut.

1979

Dudley Randall (1914–2000)

Ballad of Birmingham

*(On the Bombing of a Church in Birmingham,
Alabama, 1963)*

"Mother dear, may I go downtown
Instead of out to play,
And march the streets of Birmingham
In a Freedom March today?"

"No, baby, no; you may not go,   5
For the dogs are fierce and wild,
And clubs and hoses, guns and jail
Aren't good for a little child."

"But, mother, I won't be alone.
Other children will go with me,   10
And march the streets of Birmingham
To make our country free."

"No, baby, no, you may not go,
For I fear those guns will fire.
But you may go to church instead   15
And sing in the children's choir."

She has combed and brushed her night-dark hair,
And bathed rose petal sweet,
And drawn white gloves on her small brown hands,
And white shoes on her feet.   20

The mother smiled to know her child
Was in the sacred place,
But that smile was the last smile
To come upon her face.

For when she heard the explosion,   25
Her eyes grew wet and wild.
She raced through the streets of Birmingham
Calling for her child.

She clawed through bits of glass and brick,
Then lifted out a shoe.   30
"O here's the shoe my baby wore,
But, baby, where are you!"

1966

Edwin Arlington Robinson (1869–1935)

Richard Cory

Whenever Richard Cory went down town,
We people on the pavement looked at him:
He was a gentleman from sole to crown,
Clean favored, and imperially slim.

And he was always quietly arrayed,   5
And he was always human when he talked;
But still he fluttered pulses when he said,
"Good-morning," and he glittered when he walked.

And he was rich—yes, richer than a king—
And admirably schooled in every grace: 10
In fine, we thought that he was everything
To make us wish that we were in his place.

So on we worked, and waited for the light,
And went without the meat, and cursed the bread;
And Richard Cory, one calm summer night,   15
Went home and put a bullet through his head.

1897

Theodore Roethke (1908–1963)

My Papa's Waltz

The whiskey on your breath
Could make a small boy dizzy;
But I hung on like death:
Such waltzing was not easy.

We romped until the pans   5
Slid from the kitchen shelf;
My mother's countenance
Could not unfrown itself.

The hand that held my wrist
Was battered on one knuckle;   10
At every step you missed
My right ear scraped a buckle.

You beat time on my head
With a palm caked hard by dirt,
Then waltzed me off to bed   15
Still clinging to your shirt.

1948

William Shakespeare (1564–1616)

When, in Disgrace with Fortune and Men's Eyes

When, in disgrace with fortune and men's eyes,
I all alone beweep my outcast state,
And trouble deaf heaven with my bootless cries,
And look upon myself and curse my fate,
Wishing me like to one more rich in hope,   5
Featured like him, like him with friends possessed,
Desiring this man's art, and that man's scope,
With what I most enjoy contented least,
Yet in these thoughts myself almost despising,
Haply I think on thee, and then my state,   10
Like to the lark at break of day arising
From sullen earth, sings hymns at heaven's gate;
For thy sweet love rememb'red such wealth brings
That then I scorn to change my state with kings.

1609

Paul Simon (B. 1942)

Richard Cory

With Apologies to E. A. Robinson

They say that Richard Cory owns
One half of this old town,
With elliptical connections
To spread his wealth around.
Born into Society,   5
A banker's only child,
He had everything a man could want:
Power, grace and style.

Refrain:
But I, I work in his factory
And I curse the life I'm livin'   10
And I curse my poverty
And I wish that I could be
Oh I wish that I could be
Oh I wish that I could be
Richard Cory.   15

The papers print his picture
Almost everywhere he goes:
Richard Cory at the opera,
Richard Cory at a show
And the rumor of his party   20
And the orgies on his yacht—
Oh he surely must be happy
With everything he's got. (*Refrain.*)

He freely gave to charity,
He had the common touch,   25
And they were grateful for his patronage
And they thanked him very much,
So my mind was filled with wonder   5
When the evening headlines read:
"Richard Cory went home last night   30
And put a bullet through his head." (*Refrain.*)

                                                    1966   10

Sor Juana Inés de la Cruz (1648?–1695)

She Promises to Hold a Secret in Confidence

This page, discreetly, will convey
how, on the moment that I read it,
I tore apart your secret 15
not to let it be torn away
from me—and I will further say 5
what firm insurance followed:
those paper fragments, I also swallowed.
This secret, so dearly read—
I wouldn't want one shred
out of my chest, to be hollowed. 10

1689; trans. 2004

TRANSLATED BY DIANE THIEL

20

William Stafford (1914–1993)

Traveling through the Dark

Traveling through the dark I found a deer
dead on the edge of the Wilson River road.
It is usually best to roll them into the canyon:
that road is narrow; to swerve might make more dead.

By glow of the tail-light I stumbled back of the car   5
and stood by the heap, a doe, a recent killing;
she had stiffened already, almost cold.
I dragged her off; she was large in the belly.

My fingers touching her side brought me the reason—
her side was warm; her fawn lay there waiting,   10
alive, still, never to be born.
Beside that mountain road I hesitated.

The car aimed ahead its lowered parking lights;
under the hood purred the steady engine.
I stood in the glare of the warm exhaust turning red;   15
around our group I could hear the wilderness listen.

I thought hard for us all—my only swerving—
then pushed her over the edge into the river.

1962

25

Wallace Stevens (1879–1955)

Disillusionment of Ten O'Clock

The houses are haunted
By white night-gowns.
None are green,
Or purple with green rings,
Or green with yellow rings, 5
Or yellow with blue rings.
None of them are strange,
With socks of lace
And beaded ceintures.
People are not going 10
To dream of baboons and periwinkles.
Only, here and there, an old sailor,
Drunk and asleep in his boots,
Catches tigers
In red weather. 15

1923

Alfonsina Storni (1892–1938)

Ancestral Burden

30

You told me my father never cried
You told me my grandfather never cried.
The men of my lineage never cried
They were steel inside.

As you were saying this, you dropped a tear   5
that fell into my mouth—such poison
I have never drunk from any other cup
than this small one.

Weak woman, poor woman who understands
the ache of centuries I knew as I swallowed.   10
Oh, my spirit cannot carry
all of its load.

1919; trans. 2004

Translated by Diane Thiel

Diane Thiel (B. 1967)

Memento Mori in Middle School

When I was twelve, I chose Dante's *Inferno*
in gifted class—an oral presentation
with visual aids. My brother, *il miglior fabbro,*

said he would draw the tortures. We used ten
red posterboards. That day, for school, I dressed   5
in pilgrim black, left earlier to hang them

around the class. The students were impressed.
The teacher, too. She acted quite amused
and peered too long at all the punishments.

We knew by reputation she was cruel.   10
The class could see a hint of twisted forms
and asked to be allowed to round the room

as I went through my final presentation.
We passed the first one, full of poets cut
out of a special issue of *Horizon.*   15

The class thought these were such a boring set,
they probably deserved their tedious fates.
They liked the next, though—bodies blown about,

the lovers kept outside the tinfoil gates.
We had a new boy in our class named Paolo   20
and when I noted Paolo's wind-blown state

and pointed out Francesca, people howled.
I knew that more than one of us not-so-
covertly liked him. It seemed like hours

before we moved on to the gluttons, though,   25
where they could hold the cool fistfuls of slime
I brought from home. An extra touch. It sold

in canisters at toy stores at the time.
The students recognized the River Styx,
the logo of a favorite band of mine.   30

We moved downriver to the town of Dis,
which someone loudly re-named Dis and Dat.

And for the looming harpies and the furies,

who shrieked and tore things up, I had clipped out
the shrillest, most deserving teacher's heads   35
from our school paper, then thought better of it.

At the wood of suicides, we quieted.
Though no one in the room would say a word,
I know we couldn't help but think of Fred.

His name was in the news, though we had heard   40
he might have just been playing with the gun.
We moved on quickly by that huge, dark bird

and rode the flying monster, Geryon,
to reach the counselors, each wicked face,
again, I had resisted pasting in.   45

To represent the ice in that last place,
where Satan chewed the traitors' frozen heads,
my mother had insisted that I take

an ice-chest full of popsicles—to end
my gruesome project on a lighter note.   50
"It is a comedy, isn't it," she said.

She hadn't read the poem, or seen our art,
but asked me what had happened to the sweet,
angelic poems I once read and wrote.

The class, though, was delighted by the treat,   55
and at the last round, they all pushed to choose
their colors quickly, so they wouldn't melt.

The bell rang. Everyone ran out of school,
as always, yelling at the top of their lungs,
The *Inferno* fast forgotten, but their howls   60

showed off their darkened red and purple tongues.

2000

Memento Mori in Middle School. *Memento Mori:* Latin for "Remember you must die," the phrase now means any reminder of human mortality and the need to lead a virtuous life. 1 *Dante's* Inferno: The late medieval epic poem by the Italian poet Dante Alighieri describes a Christian soul's journey through hell. (*Inferno* means "hell" in Italian.) 3 *il miglior fabbro*: the better craftsman—Dante's term for fellow poet Daniel Arnaut, which T. S. Eliot later famously quoted to praise Ezra Pound. 15 *Horizon*: a magazine of art and culture. 20–23: *Paolo . . . Francesca*: two lovers in Dante's *Inferno* who have been damned for their adultery. 29 *River Styx*: the sacred river that flows around hell to mark its boundary. 31 *Dis*: the main city of hell named after its ruler, Dis (Pluto). 43 Geryon: a mythical three-headed, three-bodied monster Dante places in his *Inferno*.

César Vallejo (1892?–1938)

To My Brother Miguel
(in memoriam)

Brother, today I am on the bench by the house
where you leave a bottomless loss.
I remember how we would play
at this time of the day and how Mama
would lovingly chide us, "Now children."   5

Now I hide
as before, from all these evening
prayers and hope you will not find me
in the living room, the entryway, the corridors.
Later you hide, and I can't find you.   10
I remember how we made each other cry
brother—in that game.

Miguel, you disappeared
one night in August, nearly at dawn
but instead of laughing as you hid yourself,   15
you were anguished
And your twin heart of these extinguished
afternoons is weary of not finding you. Already
shadow falls on the spirit.

Listen, brother, don't be too late   20
showing up. Or Mama will fret.

1918; trans. 2004

TRANSLATED BY DIANE THIEL

Carolyn Beard Whitlow (B. 1945)

Rockin' a Man,
Stone Blind

Cake in the oven, clothes out on the line,
Night wind blowin' against sweet, yellow thighs,
Two-eyed woman rockin' a man stone blind.

Man smell of honey, dark like coffee grind;
Countin' on his fingers since last July.   5
Cake in the oven, clothes out on the line.

Mister Jacobs say he be colorblind,
But got to tighten belts and loosen ties.
Two-eyed woman rockin' a man stone blind.

Winter becoming angry, rent behind.   10
Strapping spring sun needed to make mud pies.
Cake in the oven, clothes out on the line.

Looked in the mirror, Bessie's face I find.
I be so down low, my man be so high.
Two-eyed woman rockin' a man stone blind.   15

Policemans found him; damn near lost my mind.
Can't afford no flowers; can't even cry.
Cake in the oven, clothes out on the line.
Two-eyed woman rockin' a man stone blind.

1986

Walt Whitman (1819–1892)

When I Heard the Learn'd Astronomer

When I heard the learn'd astronomer,
When the proofs, the figures, were ranged in columns before me,
When I was shown the charts and diagrams, to add, divide, and
    measure them,
When I sitting heard the astronomer where he lectured with much
    applause in the lecture-room,
How soon unaccountable I became tired and sick,   5
Till rising and gliding out I wandered off by myself,
In the mystical moist night-air, and from time to time,
Looked up in perfect silence at the stars.

1865

Richard Wilbur (B. 1921)

The Writer

In her room at the prow of the house
Where light breaks, and the windows are tossed with linden,
My daughter is writing a story.

I pause in the stairwell, hearing
From her shut door a commotion of typewriter-keys   5
Like a chain hauled over a gunwale.

Young as she is, the stuff
Of her life is a great cargo, and some of it heavy:
I wish her a lucky passage.

But now it is she who pauses,   10
As if to reject my thought and its easy figure.
A stillness greatens, in which

The whole house seems to be thinking,
And then she is at it again with a bunched clamor
Of strokes, and again is silent.   15

I remember the dazed starling
Which was trapped in that very room, two years ago;
How we stole in, lifted a sash

And retreated, not to affright it;
And how for a helpless hour, through the crack of the door, 20
We watched the sleek, wild, dark

And iridescent creature
Batter against the brilliance, drop like a glove
To the hard floor, or the desk-top.

And wait then, humped and bloody,   25
For the wits to try it again; and how our spirits
Rose when, suddenly sure,

It lifted off from a chair-back,
Beating a smooth course for the right window
And clearing the sill of the world.   30

It is always a matter, my darling,
Of life or death, as I had forgotten. I wish
What I wished you before, but harder.

1976

Miller Williams (B. 1930)

The Curator

We thought it would come, we thought the Germans would come,
were almost certain they would. I was thirty-two,
the youngest assistant curator in the country.
I had some good ideas in those days.

Well, what we did was this. We had boxes   5
precisely built to every size of canvas.
We put the boxes in the basement and waited.

When word came that the Germans were coming in,
we got each painting put in the proper box
and out of Leningrad in less than a week.   10
They were stored somewhere in southern Russia.

But what we did, you see, besides the boxes
waiting in the basement, which was fine,
a grand idea, you'll agree, and it saved the art—
but what we did was leave the frames hanging,   15
so after the war it would be a simple thing
to put the paintings back where they belonged.

Nothing will seem surprised or sad again
compared to those imperious, vacant frames.

Well, the staff stayed on to clean the rubble   20
after the daily bombardments. We didn't dream—
You know it lasted nine hundred days.
Much of the roof was lost and snow would lie
sometimes a foot deep on this very floor,
but the walls stood firm and hardly a frame fell.   25

Here is the story, now, that I want to tell you.
Early one day, a dark December morning,
we came on three young soldiers waiting outside,
pacing and swinging their arms against the cold.
They told us this: in three homes far from here   30
all dreamed of one day coming to Leningrad
to see the Hermitage, as they supposed
every Soviet citizen dreamed of doing.
Now they had been sent to defend the city,
a turn of fortune the three could hardly believe.   35

I had to tell them there was nothing to see
but hundreds and hundreds of frames where the paintings had hung.

"Please, sir," one of them said, "let us see them."
And so we did. It didn't seem any stranger
than all of us being here in the first place,   40
inside such a building, strolling in snow.

We led them around most of the major rooms,
what they could take the time for, wall by wall.
Now and then we stopped and tried to tell them
part of what they would see if they saw the paintings.   45
I told them how those colors would come together,
described a brushstroke here, a dollop there,
mentioned a model and why she seemed to pout
and why this painter got the roses wrong.

The next day a dozen waited for us,   50
then thirty or more, gathered in twos and threes.
Each of us took a group in a different direction:
Castagno, Caravaggio, Brueghel, Cézanne, Matisse,
Orozco, Manet, da Vinci, Goya, Vermeer,
Picasso, Uccello, your Whistler, Wood, and Gropper.   55
We pointed to more details about the paintings,
I venture to say, than if we had had them there,
some unexpected use of line or light,
balance or movement, facing the cluster of faces
the same way we'd done it every morning   60
before the war, but then we didn't pay
so much attention to what we talked about.
People could see for themselves. As a matter of fact
we'd sometimes said our lines as if they were learned
out of a book, with hardly a look at the paintings.   65

But now the guide and the listeners paid attention
to everything—the simple differences
between the first and post-impressionists,
romantic and heroic, shade and shadow.

Maybe this was a way to forget the war   70
a little while. Maybe more than that.
Whatever it was, the people continued to come.
It came to be called The Unseen Collection.

Here. Here is the story I want to tell you.

Slowly, blind people began to come.   75
A few at first then more of them every morning,
some led and some alone, some swaying a little.
They leaned and listened hard, they screwed their faces,
they seemed to shift their eyes, those that had them,
to see better what was being said.   80

And a cock of the head. My God, they paid attention.

After the siege was lifted and the Germans left
and the roof was fixed and the paintings were in their places,
the blind never came again. Not like before.
This seems strange, but what I think it was,   85
they couldn't see the paintings anymore.
They could still have listened, but the lectures became
a little matter-of-fact. What can I say?
Confluences come when they will and they go away.

                                            1992

William Carlos Williams (1883–1963)

The Dance

In Brueghel's great picture, The Kermess,
the dancers go round, they go round and
around, the squeal and the blare and the
tweedle of bagpipes, a bugle and fiddles
tipping their bellies (round as the thick-   5
sided glasses whose wash they impound)
their hips and their bellies off balance
to turn them. Kicking and rolling about
the Fair Grounds, swinging their butts, those
shanks must be sound to bear up under such   10
rollicking measures, prance as they dance
in Brueghel's great picture, The Kermess.

1944

William Butler Yeats (1865–1939)

The Stolen Child

Where dips the rocky highland
Of Sleuth Wood in the lake,
There lies a leafy island
Where flapping herons wake
The drowsy water-rats;   5
There we've hid our fairy vats,
Full of berries
And of reddest stolen cherries.
Come away, O human child!
To the waters and the wild   10
With a faery hand in hand,
For the world's more full of weeping than you can understand.

Where the wave of moonlight glosses
The dim grey sands with light,
Far off by furthest Rosses   15
We foot it all the night,
Weaving olden dances,
Mingling hands and mingling glances
Till the moon has taken flight;
To and fro we leap   20
And chase the frothy bubbles,
While the world is full of troubles
And is anxious in its sleep.
Come away, O human child!
To the waters and the wild   25
With a faery hand in hand,
For the world's more full of weeping than you can understand.

Where the wandering water gushes
From the hills above Glen-Car,
In pools among the rushes   30
That scarce could bathe a star,
We seek for slumbering trout
And whispering in their ears
Give them unquiet dreams;
Leaning softly out   35
From ferns that drop their tears
Over the young streams.
Come away, O human child!

To the waters and the wild
With a faery hand in hand, 40
For the world's more full of weeping than you can understand.

Away with us he's going,
The solemn-eyed:
He'll hear no more the lowing
Of the calves on the warm hillside 45
Or the kettle on the hob
Sing peace into his breast,
Or see the brown mice bob
Round and round the oatmeal-chest.
For he comes, the human child, 50
To the waters and the wild
With a faery hand in hand,
From a world more full of weeping than you can understand.

1889

The Lake Isle
of Innisfree

I will arise and go now, and go to Innisfree,
And a small cabin build there, of clay and wattles made:
Nine bean-rows will I have there, a hive for the honey-bee,
And live alone in the bee-loud glade.

And I shall have some peace there, for peace comes dropping slow,   5
Dropping from the veils of the morning to where the cricket sings;
There midnight's all a glimmer, and noon a purple glow,
And evening full of the linnet's wings.

I will arise and go now, for always night and day
I hear lake water lapping with low sounds by the shore;   10
While I stand on the roadway, or on the pavements gray,
I hear it in the deep heart's core.

1892

Credits

Whitlow, Carolyn Beard. "Rockin' a Man Stone Blind" from *Wild Meat*, Lost Roads Publishers, Providence, 1986. Copyright © 1986 by Carolyn Beard Whitlow. Reprinted by permission of the poet.

Wilbur, Richard. "The Writer," from *The Mind Reader*. Copyright © 1971 by Richard Wilbur. Reprinted by permission of Harcourt, Inc.

Williams, Miller. "The Curator," from *Adjusting to the Light*. Copyright © 1992 by Miller Williams. Reprinted by permission of the University of Missouri Press.

Williams, William Carlos. "The Dance," from *Collected Poems 1939–1962, Vol. II*. Copyright © 1944 by William Carlos Williams. Permission from New Directions Publishing Corp.

Index of Authors, Titles, and First Lines of Poems

Also by the Author

Crossroads: Creative Writing Exercises in Four Genres (2005)

Resistance Fantasies (2004)

The White Horse: A Colombian Journey (2004)

Writing Your Rhythm: Using Nature, Culture Form and Myth (2001)

Echolocations (Nicholas Roerich Prize, 2000)

Cleft in the Wall (chapbook, 1999)